FOREWORD

*irds of Paradise* tells it all! Rose Hartman has given us a fresh take on the whole process of creating fashion that comes from her up-close observation of the scene as well as her relationships with industry leaders. *Birds of Paradise* is equally rewarding for both our customers and our peers in the fashion world. And, in this game where the players are often seduced by illusions of their own making, Ms. Hartman has effectively penetrated the glamour of every event to write about the dedication and work that go into producing a new look each season, the daily hustle that a model needs to reach the top, and the kaleidoscopic vision that a photographer must bring to each new assignment. She succeeds marvelously in opening our world to the public eye—both in her writing and in her photography. These are some of the most insightful candid shots I've seen of the behind-the-scenes frenzy of fashion shows, the no-nonsense atmosphere of designers' workrooms, and the never-ending round of parties. *Birds of Paradise* adds a new dimension to fashion reporting. But most of all, the book is an alacritous celebration of the vitality that permeates the fashion world in its ultimate quest for beauty.

Egon von Fürstenberg

BIRDS OF PARADISE

AN INTIMATE VIEW OF
THE NEW YORK FASHION WORLD

BIRDS OF PARADISE

TEXT AND PHOTOGRAPHS BY

ROSE HARTMAN

A DELTA BOOK

A DELTA BOOK

Published by Dell Publishing Co., Inc.
1 Dag Hammarskjold Plaza
New York, New York 10017

Delta ® TM 755118, Dell Publishing Co., Inc.

Printed in the United States of America

First Delta printing—May 1980

Design copyright © 1980 by Hermann Strohbach

Library of Congress Cataloging in Publication Data

Hartman, Rose.
    Birds of paradise.

    (A Delta book)
    Includes index.
    1. Clothing trade—New York (City)   2. Costume
designers—New York (City)   3. Fashion.   I. Title.
TT496.U62N73   338.4'774692'097471   79-26801

ISBN 0-440-50894-0

FOR
MY MOTHER
AND
FATHER

ACKNOWLEDGMENTS

I want to thank all those who shared their insights and experiences with me, especially Ingo Thouret, Polly Allen Mellen, Kal Ruttenstein, Ray Crespin, Johnny Casablancas, Ellen Harth, Jody Donahue, Wilhelmina, Jeff Schwager, Lee Golde, Stewart Kreisler, Roz Rubenstein, Bernie Ozer, Edith Locke, Bob Currie, Candy Pratts, Larry Laslo, Carol Nussenbaum, China Machado, Daniela Morera, Terry Melville, Betsey Johnson, Carmen D'Alessio, and Richard Bernstein.

I also appreciate the assistance of Glenn Cowley, Janet Lamphier, Chris Kuppig, Toby Sullivan, Gary Luke, Carole Chazin, Robert Farber, Tui Stark, Klaus Lucka, and Yorgos Galazidis.

CONTENTS

≼INTRODUCTION≽

Who among us can resist the excitement of dressing up and becoming a bird of paradise—even for one brief moment? Who can resist the delight of removing themselves from the world of the commonplace and creating any mood they desire? Fashion can project that immediate image, whatever role or status is desired. While clothing may not make the person, it is the greatest single element in creating an initial impression that is seldom reversed.

Fashion allows us to become, temporarily, what we are not—to slip into new identities with the help of accessories, makeup, and hairstyles. Fashion enables us to camouflage our deficiencies and exaggerate our attributes. Skillful practice of fashion's subtleties can create an instant illusion of height, beauty, thinness, mystery, individuality, self-confidence, and wealth. It provides an outlet for our creative impulses, freeing us to become shimmering creatures and intoxicating presences or allowing us to blend into our surroundings. As Diana Vreeland, the high priestess of elegance, proclaimed, "Fashion is a natural delight, stronger than pestilence, war, and economic upheaval."

There is no better place in this country to observe the current mode of fashion than in New York, the fashion capital of America. No less than eighty percent of America's design concepts emanate from New York. (While many factories are scattered throughout the country, the majority of them are controlled by New York interests.)

To an outsider New York's pulsating garment center seems disorganized, frenetic, bursting at the seams. It is difficult to imagine that annually some sixty-five thousand skilled and unskilled workers manufacture clothing that wholesales for $16 billion. But these Seventh Avenue cutters, stitchers, and finishers represent only one phase of the process that begins with a designer's hazily formed idea and ends with ready-to-wear garments hanging on racks in department stores and boutiques across the country and abroad. Certainly designers' names are appearing everywhere—they have become household words—but there are many behind-the-scenes players whose efforts and expertise are vital to the finished product.

In researching *Birds of Paradise,* I spent a good deal of time reading current and back issues of American and European fashion publications as well as books written about the chiffon jungle. But the most satisfying element of my work was meeting with hundreds of key fashion people who were most generous in sharing information. Making contact with one designer would result in a meeting with a store buyer, who would in turn introduce me to a top model. This domino effect took place with startling ease, and I soon found myself on a whirlwind tour of the fashion industry. Many of the people who appear in these pages have changed positions within the industry to find new challenges. In this fast-paced world of fashion, professional titles and situations often change, almost as quick to become history as last season's styles.

But regardless of who is affiliated with whom, fashion remains the creation of illusion, fantasy, and dreams, and I realized that this finished product only results from the coordinated efforts of designers, models, publicists, fashion movers, the press, photographers, buyers, and window-display designers. Although I have only been able to write about the leading innovators in these fields, *Birds of Paradise* is really about the irrevocable, intricately orchestrated pattern of events and energies that make fashion the heady experience that it is.

New York City, August 1979   R. H.

BIRDS OF PARADISE

CHAPTER ONE

THE FASHION SHOW

YOU'RE ONLY AS GOOD AS YOUR LAST COLLECTION

It is exactly 4:00 P.M. on a winter afternoon. Halston has determined that dusk is the perfect time for showing his spring-summer made-to-order collection. As the elevator door opens on the twenty-first floor of the Olympic Towers, two attractive men in black tie approach to usher guests into the hushed atmosphere of the designer's showroom.

The setting is a narcissist's dream come true. Eighteen-foot-high mirrored doors reflect every gesture. The ceiling is nothing but light, and the red carpet is patterned with a Halston design. Clear Lucite chairs, chunky white candles, and cream-colored wild orchids (which Halston considers the sexiest of all flowers) are a perfect foil for the luxurious garments. Through the windows the midtown Manhattan skyscrapers outlined in the serene sky provide an irresistible backdrop. St. Patrick's Cathedral looms in the foreground. There is a momentary impression that mass is about to begin.

At his best Halston is both high priest and ringmaster, coordinator of the many elements that together form the ideal ambience for his refined clothes. His careful selection of each component of the show—from the soft background music to the models who parade to it—illustrates a designer's sensitivity to the creation of an image.

The elegance of the showroom is matched by the guests. Elizabeth Taylor Warner is already ensconced on the burgundy sofa in the front area reserved for visiting dignitaries. She sits next to Steve Rubell, dynamic coowner of Studio 54, one of New York's most prestigious discotheques. Other guests refrain from looking in Liz's direction; in this rarefied atmosphere celebrity eyeballing is considered gauche. As photographers immortalize her every move, Liz wraps and unwraps herself in

Melagari E. Costa's extraordinary fur creation is complemented by runway model Nancy Grigor's natural elegance.

a brilliant purple shawl. Her exquisite lavender eyes sparkle above the large gold pendant around her neck.

Halston's circle of "fashion pack" friends, like the followers of other designers in this highly competitive field, forms a support structure that extends beyond the showroom. When Liz appeared at the Academy Awards in Halston's chiffon dress with the asymmetrical neckline, she guaranteed worldwide coverage of his latest look. Not only did the American public watch her on television, but the next day millions of newspaper readers across the country saw her picture in that dress. Moreover a designer's style-conscious friends, who constantly travel and are exposed to new lines and shapes, provide him with fashion ideas long before they're even a gleam in the eye of *Women's Wear Daily.*

This coterie of intimates, composed of the designer's lovers, companions, and former classmates, is a critical part of the audience at any fashion show. They provide moral support, which is as essential to Roy Halston Frowlick as to anyone else. Members of his crowd are particularly noted for their strong concern with one another's best interests.

Heading the list of Halston's very good friends and coworkers is the amusing and cynical Elsa Peretti. Soon after entering the showroom, this talented accessory designer for Tiffany's drops her 5' 9" frame on the sofa. Her eyeglasses perching precariously on the tip of her nose, she begins gossiping with Joe Eula, an artist whose signature is frequently found on Broadway-show posters and loosely rendered illustrations of Halston's clothes. Victor Hugo, the gregarious Venezuelan responsible for the imaginative windows at Halston's Madison Avenue boutique, chats with Andy Warhol and the handful of beautiful, blasé young men hovering close to him.

One by one the fashion leaders—called simply "The Ladies" by *Women's Wear Daily*—make their entrances, many wearing the best from Halston's previous collections. These wealthy women, consummate consumers who live and breathe fashion, are escorted to their seats by sleek female assistants in black cashmere (designed by Halston, of course).

One of the first to arrive is black-lacquer-haired, whippet-boned Diana Vreeland, a former editor of *Vogue* and *Harper's Bazaar,* now director of the Costume Institute at the Metropolitan Museum of Art. "The empress of fashion" is followed by the confident Lee Radziwill, sporting huge sunglasses. (Her sister Jackie Onassis, in contrast, rarely attends fashion shows; instead she meets privately with Halston to pore over his latest sketches and fabrics.) Martha Graham, the seemingly ageless choreogra-

Top model Billie Blair struts down the runway in Anne Klein evening pajamas.

Jeremy Wren (told to *WWD*): "Clothing are like children to their designers; it's devastating when they're not shown correctly."

pher, enters bundled in sumptuous sable and wearing a gold lamé turban. Next comes tawny-haired Ethel Scull, the Pop Art collector, wearing a Broadway bow tie and a beautifully cut white suit. Meanwhile fashion maven Daniela Morera looks dazzling as she and *Interview* cover designer Richard Bernstein comment on last night's dinner party and make plans for this evening's festivities: supper at Halston's townhouse, then nonstop dancing at Studio 54.

Since fashion shows are invariably jam-packed, only those fortunate enough to be store presidents, top buyers, and powerful members of the press get an unobstructed view from carefully marked front-row seats. But buyers aren't invited to Halston's made-to-order show. Here private customers order clothes costing from $1,250 to $2,500 directly from one of his assistants; a select few attend Halston's intimate lunches and discuss their latest choices with him. And unlike most shows, which are crowded and hot, the environment here is calm and controlled. Yet no matter how uncomfortable a site may be, fashion addicts—professional and otherwise—pour in not only to see a designer's new line but to indulge in one of their favorite pastimes: hawk-eyed observation and exchange of confidences. They admire an editor who wraps mink tails insouciantly around her delicate throat, a socialite who belts narrow multicolored ribbons around a cream-colored cashmere dress, an Italian photographer with one tiny diamond in her ear who wears silver-gray stiletto-heeled boots. Although there may be tension between members of the audience, they greet one another with delicately placed kisses on upturned faces (definitely a carry-over from attending showings in Paris, Florence, and Milan).

But this show, like every other, will not begin until the key media people arrive; designers have been known to delay their presentations until the entrance of *Women's Wear Daily*. Members of the press file in accompanied by photographers overloaded with cameras and lighting equipment to catch the clothes fully accessorized.

Vogue editor-in-chief Grace Mirabella, elegant in brown Ultrasuede, enters. She drops a leather pouch onto the floor of the otherwise pristine studio and takes out a tiny notebook. Bernadine Morris of *The New York Times,* looking understated as usual, sits down nearby.

As guests finally settle into their seats, soft Brazilian music begins.

Miguel Cruz's luxurious furs.

Prepared by a free-lance coordinator to set the low-key tone of the show, it reflects Halston's awareness that the mind-blasting sound of the early 1970s is best left to others. Others like Kenzo, for example, who opened a boutique at Bloomingdale's and held his show at Studio 54 for some eight hundred guests. The Japanese designer's audience went wild watching the models prancing and flirting up and down the runway, scattering confetti and hundreds of brightly colored balloons in a roaring finale punctuated by disco queen Grace Jones singing "La Vie en Rose."

But in the plush Fifth Avenue showroom that Halston casually admits is "in the million-dollar area," nothing distracts from the clothes. There is no commentator to interrupt the flow of the presentation. Twenty years ago such an omission would have been unthinkable; but since the innovative English designer Mary Quant dispensed with commentary in the early 1960s, most fashion shows do without. Pauline Trigère is the exception. In a nonstop monologue she gently cajoles, charms, and propels her models along as she describes the exciting possibilities her exquisitely tailored clothes offer a woman of unlimited means.

Every fashion show revolves around an idea employed to catch the audience's attention. As Halston's models move regally down the runway, the clothes begin to spell out the designer's new night-flier theme: billowing dresses that fill the air like parachutes with each step the models take. Designers rehire these catwalk stars (with the addition of two or three newcomers every season) because of their ability to modify their appearances and project an instant magnetism that enhances whatever they wear. Before a show begins, designers tell their models what attitude to convey. Sant'Angelo encourages them to evoke the freedom and fun of a circus while moving down the runway. Stephen Burrows's models sway to a Latin dance step that he teaches them. Oscar de la Renta likes them to suggest whispering taffeta and fine lace, while Trigère opts for a mature, worldly look, and Blass's preference is American Yachting Club. Fernando Sanchez encourages open sensuality; Perry Ellis likes a disarming, playful style; Kenzo chooses flamboyant, high-spirited models who take center stage and play it for all it's worth; Yves St. Laurent's models dip and whirl.

Now Karen Bjornson, icy-hard, golden, and one of Halston's favorite models, glides along the runway. For one magical instant she is immortal—a delicately carved marble figure for whom ordinary day-to-day activities are inconceivable. More models appear in exquisite clothes. Some pout; others are defiant or aloof, and one or two are open, almost friendly. But regardless of their personalities, all respond equally well to the photographers' insistent whispers to pause and turn once more.

Models onstage during Anne Klein's show.

As the show continues, the audience falls increasingly under Halston's carefully orchestrated yet seemingly effortless spell. Lee Radziwill takes notes; she already knows that Halston has outdone himself. She might be ordering the casual bias-cut linen suit and several of his dazzling gowns and pajamas in eye-opening shades of red, purple, and lime green.

Enthusiasm mounts as Billie Blair makes her head-turning entrance. She has already begun strutting fifteen feet before she hits the runway, gathering the necessary momentum that makes her entrance so compelling. Billie is a hardworking professional. She knows that she, too, is a star—one of those women whose aura, carriage, and height make her an unrivaled vehicle for maximizing the effect of any garment she might wear. As she moves, her silk-screened chiffon gown seems to fly from her body. The audience applauds. Even Liz Taylor whispers, "I wish I were as gorgeous as the clothes and the models."

Carla Araque, an aristocratic, fine-boned beauty with jet-black hair and an ivory complexion, parades by in a stunning red harem-bottomed cashmere gown (cashmere has always been Halston's forte). The designer invariably puts Carla in red, because he knows that color is "simply divine" on her.

All fashion shows follow the same general pattern. Beginning with casual wear, they move to "after five" and big evenings, then culminate in a burst of fantasy—a diaphanous wedding gown, a black satin tuxedo, a jewel-encrusted dress. Halston's grand finale features Liza Minnelli, another of his close friends, striding down the runway to her latest hit song in a flawless flesh-and-black satin gown.

At the close of the show the models emerge together like multihued birds of paradise, hovering for one brief moment before disappearing into the darkness. There is a burst of bravos, and Halston appears from behind the scenes in a black suit (the only other color he wears is white) with his collar turned up stylishly, a flawless turtleneck, and dark glasses that conceal months of tension.

Once again Halston has successfully gauged the mood of his potential and current clients, all of whom exude self-confidence, who want to be stylish but not showy. Halston's women save their extravagant clothes for private homes, yachts, and resorts. Now private customers congratulate him. The fashion press gives him rave reviews. Waiters offer platters of smoked salmon, steak tartar, and ladyfinger biscuits. Only one flaw marks the celebration. As Minnelli embraces Taylor, a silver tray of Dom Perignon champagne in Tiffany crystal glasses falls to the floor, brushing Liz's boot. She flashes a devastating glance at the rapidly retreating figure of the guilty waiter.

Bethann Hardison: "I brought theatricality and salesmanship to runway modeling. The roar of the crowd encouraged me. When I first started I seemed unfriendly and stern as a reaction to racial prejudice."

The crowd disperses. Clutching red-grosgrained-tied white boxes filled with Halston's overnight-success fragrance, the guests marvel at his uncanny ability to give each woman what she wants—whether it's Ultrasuede, an asymmetrical neckline, uncluttered cashmere sweater-dresses, dazzling beaded gowns—even before she realizes that she wants it.

After receiving the accolades of press, buyers, and friends, any Seventh Avenue designer is left with only one question: "Did they write?" In other words did the buyers jot down the style numbers listed on the program to refer to on a subsequent visit to the designer's showroom? How many asked for appointments to order clothes in the upcoming weeks?

Although designers of the stature of a Halston, Blass, or Beene can withstand a bad review, they are decidedly among the minority. An aspiring designer's hopes for fame can easily be broken by a single unsuccessful show. One beginner who was to discover this for herself was the young Princess Diane de Beauvau.

The princess comes from a family whose name appears in European history books; her grandfather, Antenor Patino, is a multimillionaire tin magnate. Bored with her studies, de Beauvau came to New York by way of Paris to participate in the pulsating world called fashion. Launching her apprenticeship as Halston's executive assistant, she observed the complicated inner machinations of the industry. When she wasn't working, she was partying with Halston's sybaritic friends and being photographed for the cover of Andy Warhol's *Interview,* a monthly magazine devoted to art, entertainment, society, and semi-intimate small talk. Six months later, with the generous backing of Philippine socialite Maria Fores, the twenty-two-year-old princess decided to set out on her own.

As de Beauvau's collection developed, fashion observers noted that a number of garments strongly resembled those designed by her former employer; the similarities included fabrics, silhouettes, and colors. As rumors spread, the media had a field day reporting that Halston was about to sue de Beauvau for $25,000. Although it is not uncommon for assistants to strike out on their own, it is unpleasant when a former apprentice's first collection revolves about the ideas of her mentor.

De Beauvau staged her first fashion show on a stormy Monday. Eager

Marion York (Yorkie) at The Pines before her appearance on the runway.

to see whether she was the "new St. Laurent," as a reputable fashion editor described this intrepid entrant in a game where stakes are usually double or nothing, hundreds of "beautiful people," celebrities, and members of the media filled the main ballroom of the Plaza Hotel. The Patinos, who flew in from Paris to witness the collection, were seated front and center, next to Diana Vreeland. Moving to deafening disco music, spectacular models—the best in the business—showed poorly constructed clothes and crass copies of Halston's easily identifiable designs.

A few days later de Beauvau was interviewed in her elegant Fifty-seventh Street showroom for *Der Spiegel,* a German publication resembling *Time* magazine. Except for several seamstresses the showroom was deserted—a far cry from the usual hubbub that follows a presentation. Although the German journalist later described de Beauvau as a "wunderkind," the New York press was considerably less appreciative: the fashion dailies noted that a glittering audience is not enough to ensure a successful collection.

The buyers, in total agreement with the fashion press, avoided de Beauvau. (In any event, when *Women's Wear Daily* pans a designer, it is a rare buyer who ignores its negative judgment.) Halston's pending suit against de Beauvau, along with the reviews and the poor quality of her designer-priced clothes, ensured total failure. Two months later a telephone call to de Beauvau's showroom was answered by a recorded message: "I'm sorry. This number is temporarily disconnected."

Although the outcome of de Beauvau's ambitions was bleak, it was not totally devastating. Backer Maria Fores could easily afford to find another project, and Halston, one of the most successful American fashion entrepreneurs in history, magnanimously dropped his suit. In fact the princess was subsequently seen at a Halston fashion show wearing her usual basic black and looking a little more worldly.

In contrast a single fashion show can generate enough momentum to make it all more than worthwhile. If an inventive collection of clothes or accessories receives enough favorable press coverage, specialty shops may decide to promote the creator, and a fashion director may establish a boutique for the designer within a department store. Judi Buie's Boot Shop at Serendipity, a popular New York restaurant-cum-boutique, is a case in point. Before Texas boots became the rage in 1977, most boot lovers chose the durable Frye brand. In a one-shot effort to ignite a desire for custom-made boots in exotic skins like turtle, ostrich, and iguana, Buie employed Roz Rubenstein, an innovative young publicist, to produce a fashion show. Twelve years in the fashion industry enabled Ruben-

Karen Bjornson models a Ralph Lauren design.

stein to borrow clothes and furs from top designers who were more than willing to support a hot item that might enhance their creations and provide them with publicity (generally designers help one another only when they are in noncompetitive fields). She also enlisted a number of her famous friends to model thirty different kinds of boot. New York City ballet star and dance teacher Jacques D'Amboise leaped down the stairs; Michel Stuart, of the Broadway hit *Chorus Line*, masked his face with a photograph; Tommy Tune danced joyously; Sylvia Miles smiled and paraded center stage. In a jet-black Halston cape, Sant'Angelo's silk-scarf gown, or Fiorucci's trend-setting clothes, the models clearly projected the show's message: "I'm wearing Texas cowboy boots with . . ."

This brilliantly conceived event launched a new style. The hundreds of fashion mavens who attended happily accepted the photocopied programs, which perfectly suited the setting—The Lone Star Café, a casual

Models making themselves
up before a show.

Pat Cleveland, superstar runway model, adjusting her outfit before presenting Oscar de la Renta's fashions.

Greenwich Village restaurant famed for Texas chili and country-and-western music. The press loved it. Eugenia Sheppard began her "Inside Fashion" column in the *New York Post* with the line, "Every woman should have a cowboy in her life at some time, and if she can't get the cowboy, at least she can manage the boots." And Buie is a very happy lady who can barely keep her Tony Lamas and Dixon boots in stock.

When thunderous applause sweeps the room at the end of a show, months of sleepless nights, nervous preparations, indigestion, and fear of failure evaporate. Designers willingly spend an average of $5,000 to present a collection because they know that a strong impact can skyrocket a career. To elicit favorable responses, a show must capture the imagination of the overworked press and the buyers who attend seven or eight a day. Perry Ellis once imported a team of Princeton cheerleaders, and

Bethann Hardison: "So much communication is possible on the runway; you can warm someone's heart."

Betsey Johnson played punk rock tapes in St. Clement's Church while models of every shape and size added and subtracted body-hugging separates.

Every detail counts. Accessories, for example, make a subtle but important contribution to the overall effect of a fashion show. Once a collection is complete, the designer and his assistants carefully consider what shoes will best accentuate which dresses, which neckline will need a scarf, pin, or flower. Accessories such as shoes, hats, and jewelry are usually borrowed; the lender gets a credit line in the show's program. Young accessory designers yearn for exposure and are delighted to lend their talents to other designers. Often an accessory will be dyed to complement a particular outfit. If the color change doesn't satisfy the designer's expectations, he is faced with the added pressure of searching the city at the last minute for buttons that will perfectly match an aubergine-velvet cropped jacket or an ivory linen nautical coat. Occasionally, if a designer needs props to dramatize a particular garment, he may hire a free-lance stylist to find the perfect walking stick or antique telescope. In one show top model Alva Chinn, blade thin as ever, modeled a Halston print dress with her month-old silk-diapered baby tucked under her arm.

Choosing a setting for the show is particularly challenging. With the help of a publicist a designer seeks a location that is suitable both in mood and in price and that will contribute to the desired ambience. One season, when Bill Blass chose The Four Seasons, the exquisitely clad models were required to move gingerly around the restaurant's indoor pool. Diane Von Furstenberg almost overwhelmed her rather casual wrap dresses by showing them in the chic ballroom of the Pierre Hotel. Willie Smith aired his sporty separates in an enormous art gallery in Manhattan's SoHo district, while Bill Kaiserman displayed his neutral-toned sexy clothes in the pulsating, rainbow-lit Studio 54. Clovis Ruffin rented the old Edison Theater to show a delicate, understated line (momentarily marred by a rapid live S & M scene). Regina Kravitz opted for the New York Squash Club to counterpoint her glamorous Retro clothes; Paul Ropp selected an African artifacts gallery as a foil for his brilliantly colored Indian fashions; and Armani chose Xenon (the club that almost usurped Studio 54's popularity) to show his elegant collection.

When the location, date, and time have been determined, the publicist

Ingo, one of the top international male models, parades before an audience at a fund-raising fashion show at The Pines on Fire Island.

mails a press release or invitation to buyers, newspapers, magazines, and important private customers to be sure that the appropriate people attend. While the designer concentrates on the creative end, his assistants work out the numerous preparatory details. Chairs must be rented, security guards hired, and transportation ensured for the staff and clothing if the collection is to be seen outside of the showroom; liquor and food may be ordered. Some consider the use of flowers "gilding the lily"; others insist on exotic plants or gigantic bouquets of seasonal flowers. The simplest or most lavish site can be made more exciting by a creative disc jockey, lighting expert, or choreographer to create special movements for the models.

Although Charles Suppon was fortunate enough to recruit his old friend Peter Allen to play "I Love New York" during his fashion show with a New York theme, the standard approach is to hire a disc jockey to supervise tapes or records. Generally a designer describes the mood of the show to the disc jockey, who makes the preliminary selections. Some designers inspire disc jockeys with consecutive sketches of the clothes to be shown, whereas others, such as Richard Assatly and Bill Kaiserman, have invited them to view the collection. The lighting technician, who also uses his skills to enhance the clothes, can adjust his colors to produce increasingly dramatic effects as the show reaches its climax. When Milanese designer Gianni Versace showed at the Pierre, a barrage of spotlights, reminiscent of a Hollywood premiere, crisscrossed over the models as they paraded by in tight formation. The number of models in a show is determined by the size of the production, the budget, and the room; as few as eight or as many as eighteen may be hired. Once the models are selected, they are asked to try on various outfits. As they move around in the sample clothes, the designer decides who will wear what. Alterations are made to ensure a perfect fit for each individual.

Most designers demand a dress rehearsal, complete with lights, music, and cues, on the day of the presentation. Each entrance and exit is precisely timed to avoid long pauses; in a typical show a model should take approximately one minute to show a garment. She will come out alone, as one of a pair, or, in some instances, as a member of a group to emphasize a designer's statement.

Models receive help in presenting themselves and the designer's concepts. Backstage, detailed sketches or photos of complete outfits are placed near each model's clothing rack. Clothes are assembled in categories; the appropriate hat, jewelry, or scarf is found hanging by the garment in a plastic bag or in a large bin nearby. Shoes are stored in boxes

Models backstage at Bill Kaiserman's show, waiting to go out on the runway.

near the individual rack. Students who want to learn every phase of the fashion business, members of a designer's staff, or—if the event is low-budgeted, friends who understand the designer's intentions—work together to produce a smoothly run show.

When a fabric trade association, a group of fashion executives, or a charity invites thirty or forty designers to show their latest creations in a ballroom or large restaurant, professional dressers are usually hired to ease the models in and out of their outfits. A good dresser is an invaluable asset; working closely with the model, she helps her change clothes as effortlessly and quickly as possible. The chief dresser generally will be paid $45 for three hours, while her assistant will make about $25 for the same amount of time. Each one is assigned specific models, whose runway appearances should be spaced far enough apart to avoid the dresser's nightmare of putting a garment on a model backward or out of sequence.

Considering the high level of excitement and pressure before and during a show, it is not unusual for tempers to flare. Clara Johnson, a freelance dresser for the past thirty years, has learned how to cope with tension. "If a model is uptight or nervous and doesn't want to be dressed by me, I don't take her moods personally. Instead I try to find out what's wrong. If a designer complains that I don't work fast enough for him, he either won't call me again or I'll refuse to work for him," she explains philosophically. "Designers are all a pain in the neck until they know who's working for them. You must remember that their clothes are their babies. When French or Italians come here, they're very nervous; they can't imagine anyone except a French or Italian doing anything right."

Last-minute hysteria caused by a model's late arrival or the misplacement of a bracelet, a boot, or a hat prevents most shows from beginning on time. But like a Broadway show, once it begins, there is no stopping it. Each time a model dashes backstage to change, bedlam breaks loose. Models shout to their dressers, "These boots don't fit properly." "I can't find the other amethyst earring." "The hem just ripped." "Where's that veil?" The dresser unzips, unbuttons, unbuckles the model's clothes, then helps her into the next garment. A makeup expert—taking his or her color cues from the designer—freshens or reapplies makeup while a hair stylist magically creates flowing curls that will soon be replaced by a glamorous chignon ornamented with a delicate tortoiseshell comb. Elsewhere in the room one model is applying blood-red nail polish while another frantically searches for a dropped lapis lazuli pendant; an assistant tilts a broad-brimmed fedora ever so slightly. A sewer is on hand to repair an unraveled hem or popped button seconds before the model reaches the

Pat Cleveland modeling in Halston's cathedral-like showroom.

runway. Sometimes the designer decides to make a last-minute change, attaching an organdy rose to the lapel of a wool suit or adding a straw boater to a gauzy casual dress.

The starter is another key person who ensures a fast-moving show. Standing near the runway, the starter (usually an in-house publicist or a designer's assistant) frantically summons the models, checks their appearance, and paces the show. A good starter knows that too many pauses between models may sour a prospective buyer, who affects the bottom line in the actualization of the designer's dreams.

Even though everyone involved in producing a fashion show tries to make it as flawless as possible, things often do go wrong. When Charles Suppon worked for Calvin Klein, they barely slept for twelve days preceding each show. On one occasion, Suppon recalls, "We had taken Polaroids and charted all the outfits. At the last minute we discovered that a box of precisely coordinated jewelry and hats was missing. Then two Polaroids got mixed up, so the models wore the wrong outfits; one put on low heels, which made the pants she wore too long. During the finale, as the theme from *Chinatown* began, every model, or 'bridesmaid,' wanted to make a separate grand entrance instead of the group entrance we had planned. And last but not least the single calla lily carried by the bride accidentally got ripped. Although the show was a great success, it was the last time that Calvin didn't have a dress rehearsal."

When Julio previewed his collection at his opulent Fifty-second Street mansion, he was overwhelmed by an enormous crowd of fashion aficionados surging past the security guard. Distracted by showing clothes on two floors, the models inadvertently overlooked one room filled with restless buyers, who left angrily and saw the collection at the showroom later that week. The next season Julio held his show at the New York Athletic Club, a bastion of WASP propriety.

A prop once went wild at Oscar de la Renta's showroom when Modigliani-like Pat Cleveland emerged in a tropical print dress with a gorgeous parrot poised on her arm. Frightened by the photographers' nonstop strobes, the bird suddenly clawed the model's wrist. Cleveland screamed, cursed under her breath, and watched helplessly as the parrot zoomed madly around the room to the delight of the usually cynical photographers.

At Mary McFadden's show at Circle in the Square photographers who thought that models in sumptuous black evening dresses were signaling the end of the show rushed across the stage and ignored the gold-clad bride as she made an all-too-brief entrance.

Bill Kaiserman's beauties backstage before the show.

Minutes before Charles Jourdan's fashion show was to begin at Studio 54, an entire shipment of the world's sexiest shoes was stolen. Luckily the situation was salvaged by a strong slide presentation and the tightly choreographed group of dancers hired as models. As the dancers went through their routines in rehearsal shoes, the audience viewed the slides.

The Rainbow Room high above Rockefeller Center was the scene of another catastrophic fashion event. A huge crowd watching the D. D. Dominick collection suddenly found itself sitting in a darkened room. A television crew dismantling its equipment after shooting a portion of the show accidentally shut all the lights, and no one could reactivate the centrally controlled source. As the unflappable models moved down the staircase as if nothing unusual had happened, assistants backstage scrambled around in the dark screaming for the shawls, hair ornaments, and espadrilles needed to accessorize the clothes.

And when Bill Kaiserman used the mammoth passenger terminal at New York City's Pier 54 for his spring showing, he thoughtfully chartered buses to whiz press and buyers to designer Charles Suppon's show afterward. In the usual madness surrounding any show (in this case last-minute clothing deliveries from Italy required round-the-clock fittings), a certified check for the bus drivers had been overlooked. The fact that Kaiserman grosses $10 million a year in men's and women's wear and is a member of the Coty Hall of Fame meant little to the drivers. By the time they were convinced of Kaiserman's credibility and accepted his personal check, the slightly inconvenienced editors and buyers had already found taxis along Twelfth Avenue and managed to get to the Fashion Institute of Technology where an anxious Suppon was waiting.

For a designer the anxiety rarely lets up. Whether his last show was extravagant or run on a tight budget, marred by mistakes or perfectly executed, he is at work on his next collection before the celebration of the last has died away. "What will I do next season?" is the designer's constant question, and the fashion world perpetually awaits his answer.

Cesar Barro shows one of Egon Von Furstenberg's more extravagant designs.

CHAPTER TWO

THE DESIGNER

THE NEW
CELEBRITY

"It might be good for designers to leave the industry and travel for a while, let their minds clear, but none of them is willing to give up their dynasties."

—A free-lance Photographer

New York's fashion industry, a heady extravaganza of commerce and creativity, is packed into less than one square mile in and around Seventh Avenue. From Monday to Friday the garment center teems with fast-talking manufacturers, sleek models dragging huge tote bags, harried salesmen, high-keyed buyers, ambitious designers. The sidewalks overflow with workers unloading double-parked trucks or pushing unwieldy racks of clothes. Inside the nondescript buildings are high-tech showrooms as well as tiny offices decorated with shoddy furniture and plastic plants, and on-premises workrooms where anonymous patternmakers, cutters, and dressmakers labor, producing everything from swimsuits to snowsuits, evening gowns to bathrobes.

In this volatile, male-dominated environment, which encompasses both high fashion and mass merchandising, vast fortunes are made and lost overnight. The welfare of thousands depends on whether shoppers across the country will indulge themselves in a new dress or blouse or pair of pants—and on who has produced the garments they will buy. Their decisions may be influenced by a designer's reputation, the quality of the clothes, or the impact of an advertisement, and their decisions definitely will be making money for someone on Seventh Avenue.

Without the designer none of this could exist. And without talent the designer could not exist. But innate creativity is not enough: a designer's ultimate success rests on a combination of intelligence and instinct, a knowledge of manufacturing, marketing, and finance, plus a talent for creating clothes that women with different body types can wear. Unable to be all things to all customers, a savvy designer pinpoints the person who will respond to his particular look: a career woman with a thriving so-

Regina Kravitz fits her model Kristie in preparation for an upcoming show.

cial life, a married woman with a large family, a college student, or a fashion trendsetter who jets to the right places at the right times of year. He senses whether they want more of the same or are ready for a radical change, and he gives them what they want whether or not they know they want it.

A designer must have a wide range of skills that enables him to choose a staff compatible with his fashion philosophy; order the most interesting fabrics in the right colors; contend with embargoes in India, strikes in Italy, the loss of a shipment at the airport; endure endless meetings with business managers to review fabric, trimming, freight, and labor costs; hire skilled cutters who can manipulate the newest textiles; supervise production to maintain the high standards of his painstakingly constructed

Geoffrey Beene: "The best way to be noticed in the U.S. is to move to Europe. My business has doubled since I opened in Milan."

Stephen Burrows: "Seventh Avenue is concerned with a price point; everything is brown and boring; they're interested in making polyester clothes that women can throw into their washing machines and put on. Everything is too serious on SA. People on Seventh Avenue are stylists, not designers."

samples; deal with the sudden closing of a factory staffed with expert embroiderers; indulge in time-consuming experimentation (if a new button is desired, a mold must be made and at least a thousand ordered); endure backbiting and lack of cooperation among competitors who are less than willing to share resources; anticipate how many yards of that never-to-be-forgotten print are necessary to accommodate buyers' requests for more garments. Moreover the designer must determine which stores will carry his collections; ensure that clothes will not leave the warehouse improperly sewn or pressed; cope with overcutting and the cancellation of orders for goods that are not delivered on time. And he must worry about the quantity and quality of press coverage for his latest collection; make certain that a favorite model is available for fittings; fulfill his business-related social commitments; try to control his increasing panic as the date of a show looms nearer; and wonder where he'll find enough time to do everything. As Diane Von Furstenberg admitted to *Women's Wear Daily*, "I need air. I'm suffocating because my whole life is a schedule." Adds Donna Karan of Anne Klein, "To survive and be creative is a job in itself."

Like artists, designers function full time, reflecting society as it is today and as it will be tomorrow. At the same time that they contend with daily production and distribution problems, they are looking ahead, collecting ideas and images. Exposed to similar stimuli, they tend to reject what is too familiar and boring. Like hothouse flowers, top-flight designers respond to the slightest social change and telegraph their message to a fashion-hungry audience.

Current life-styles motivate changing fashion, and contemporary designers have responded to increased mobility, more casual views of sexuality, and the current preoccupation with the body beautiful—roller skating, disco dancing, jogging, health spas. The trend toward "Everything shows, anything goes" is exemplified by sexy, second-skin styles made of the new synthetics (polyurethane, Spandex, parachute nylon) and back-slit skirts, cinched waists, and tottering heels.

Designers go to the same films, art shows, ballets, dinners, discos, resorts, and restaurants; they frequent the same neighborhoods (Christo-

pher Street's predominantly homosexual population invariably offers
Seventh Avenue men's wear designers the latest fashion statement) and
read the same publications. Alert to the subtle pulse of change, they absorb the aesthetic, social, economic, technological, and political climate
with a heightened awareness. A charismatic personality, an antique wallpaper motif, a nationwide craze, the women's movement, an antique jacket spotted in a thrift shop—all have been reflected at one time or another
in new silhouettes and accessories.

Whenever a designer feels stifled by business details, he turns to travel

Perry Ellis: "Sexual preference has little to do with design concepts."

Designer Geoffrey Beene at a Coty Awards presentation
held at the Fashion Institute of Technology.

Pat Cleveland: "Halston is a smart businessman type of designer who knows how to drape and hide anyone's faults. A designer's home and life-style reveal a lot about a designer's sensibility. Halston is completely modern. Valentino has peacocks roaming through his gardens in Rome; he's a great romantic."

for an endless source of stimuli. On the road Giorgio Sant'Angelo fills notebooks with observations, sketches, photos, and postcards for later reference. On his last trip to Bali he concentrated on the people's lives—their dance, the way they washed their clothes, how they wore their sarongs. His research resulted in multilayered, brilliantly colored jackets, and seductive, glittery evening dresses. And when Mary McFadden lived in South Africa, primitive neckpieces and native clothing inspired her own body-hugging clothes and striking jewelry. Last year McFadden took a thirty-eight-thousand mile, fifteen-day trip to thirty-four countries in search of influences for subsequent design.

Other designers look to the past. The fringed and buckled western heroes and heroines who populated young Ralph Lauren's dreams as he sat years ago in a Bronx movie theater recently resurfaced in his updated version of Americana. Clothing styles he admired in old English films were resurrected in a recent collection as contemporary tweedy jackets. ("They're now being copied by Brooks Brothers," Lauren says, "although they'd never admit it.") In contrast Kenzo told *W,* "I am not going to the South Seas. I am not going to the Wild West. I am through with themes."

Rather than using any specific theme or locale, Bill Kaiserman designs for an imaginary perfect woman. One season she was an aloof ultrasophisticate who went to the best places; he took her to the "limits of sensuality" through tailored, sexy clothes. When Calvin Klein sits down to sketch, he conjures up an image of Katharine Hepburn or the sleek career woman Faye Dunaway played in *Network.* A thousand-year-old prayer stone in his favorite oval shape, one of his prized possessions, is clearly reflected in the packaging of his cosmetic line and the soft shawl collar of his best-selling blouses.

Oscar de la Renta's ideal is a self-assured woman who loves extravagant parties. When avowed disco fanatic Stephen Burrows watches a woman dance, a dress that embodies her movements immediately appears in his head; his sensuous evening dresses have earned him the title, "the king of cling." He gets ideas from constant television viewing as well as from simply observing the kind of woman who feels free enough to wear his slinky, revealing clothes.

Etta Froio (*WWD* fashion editor): "We've all heard that designers hate women. Any designer is in business to make money, and he wants women to look beautiful. The idea that these are men who hate women is ridiculous."

Halston is inspired not by one woman, but by all females—from reed-like nymphs to ample-figured movie queens. When he worked at Bergdorf's early in his career, he realized that society women—his predominant clientele—wanted to look anonymous during the day and extravagant at home or with their equally wealthy friends at night. To accommodate them Halston provided clothes that were simple yet refined enough to become backdrops for their sumptuous jewels. On the other hand Diane Von Furstenberg's awareness of working women's needs for sensible clothes resulted in her basic wrapped dress. "When we're young, we can wear jeans and be Communists," she told a fashion reporter, "but when we have children and assume important positions in the world, we have to look respectable."

Many designers are motivated by the feel or look of a fabric. Donna Karan visits European fabric markets, where she determines the mood of her next season's line before returning to New York to collaborate with her partner, Louis Dell'Olio. Halston runs a piece of cloth across his cheek to see how it will feel on the body. Carol Horn hunts for unorthodox fabrics that can work for her. As she told *Cosmopolitan,* "I found this loose woolly hopsacking that another designer had put down; he called it beggar's cloth. I jumped at the stuff and made the house confine its sales to me."

Most American designers will not readily admit that they are sometimes influenced by Europeans (who show their collections earlier), by old masters like Charles James, Chanel, and Dior, and by each other; nevertheless it was rumored that at a dress rehearsal for a group show a leading designer took photographs of a rival's collection. It is not difficult to understand why: the pressure to turn an inspiration, whatever its source, into a complete new collection begins as soon as the last collection is shown.

To create a prophetic look stressing a new shape, color, or sense of proportion, a designer will begin by making sketches; if he cannot draw, a creative assistant will illustrate his ideas. Often, displeased with the results, he will discard fifty or even one hundred drawings and perhaps begin to fear that he's run out of ideas. Then, suddenly, a seemingly

Giorgio Sant'Angelo congratulates Betsey Johnson after her highly successful show.

Ray Crespin: "Ralph Lauren's strength is his entire look, top to bottom; otherwise, you lose the power of his collection. Calvin Klein's clothes have mobility and can be worn with anyone else's."

meaningless event—perhaps a glimpse of a lean and smiling bellhop in an exquisitely tailored jacket—may spark his creativity. Excited, he begins to draw square-shouldered, body-hugging cropped jackets until he is satisfied with the shape. As a final touch he adds gold-braid edging and glittering buttons. He might pause to ask his assistant for feedback or work uninterrupted until the core of the next collection emerges. The new fitted, slightly flared silhouette moves from short-jacketed suits to skirts, dresses, coat-dresses, evening tunics over pants in four or five key colors and textures. The designer browses through swatch books or chooses the most advanced fabrics from an earlier visit to the European trade shows. Oscar de la Renta admitted to *WWD,* "I buy more Italian than French. For the quality the Italians have the best prices." Seeking those colors and materials that will dramatize his new silhouette (the right fabric can create a sensational look even when the line or cut is less than memorable), he may create cashmere and wool samples for day, reserving for night heavy satins and velvets in rich, regal colors.

The realization of a collection generally begins with the designer draping and pinning a piece of muslin or last year's fabric on a mannequin or, as women designers often do, on herself. According to Betsey Johnson, "I'm my own customer; I have to move with the clothes. If I worked in muslin, I'd know what muslin was like, but not what the cloth does." Similarly Norma Kamali searches for fabric until she finds something that really hits her. As she told *Viva,* "I stand in front of a mirror and play with it, and all of a sudden I see something. A certain part of it looks right. It's both fighting against and working with it at the same time. I almost don't feel in control of it . . . It's the biggest high when you get that, when all of a sudden something is there. I finish and then I'm looking for the next high, another piece of fabric. I can get neurotic about it, but I love it."

When a large collection is in the works, two or three technical assistants will help the designer "drape" the sketches—pin the fabric to a mannequin and cut a pattern from it. They will continue pinning and re-pinning, widening or narrowing a sleeve, curving or slanting a neckline, raising or lowering a waist half an inch until the muslin form is ready to be made into a pattern. At this point a highly skilled sample maker will

Calvin Klein.

prepare the original, which ultimately will be fitted on the model designated to wear it in the upcoming show. Givenchy told a fashion reporter, "My mannequins are very important. They wear the clothes. During the fittings, their movements, gestures, attitudes, tell me something. If they don't feel right, it doesn't work."

Each garment undergoes the same meticulous treatment until there are enough to constitute a collection of thirty to one hundred fifty pieces. When the samples are assembled, a designer and his capable young assistant (who also orders fabrics for production and does research in libraries looking for new ideas), edit the line. Clothes that are too outrageous or too repetitive are rejected; the economy-minded production staff drops styles that cost too much to produce or seem to have little sales potential. The resulting collection combines safe, saleable shapes—new versions of best sellers—with several headline-making designs that indicate an anticipation of what customers will want.

Once the collection is aired, only those pieces that buyers order will be put into production; out of one hundred fifty items, two thirds may go into production as is or in slightly altered form. Dresses shown on the runway are designed for a 5' 9" or 5' 10" model and exaggerated for impact. When Claude Montana shows in Paris, one sees superwomen with oversized shoulders and tiny waists; to reach a larger audience, he alters the original shape prior to production. The degree of modification varies. Some designers are unwilling to change their clothes for buyers; others alter the length, specify slits, narrow armhole closings, or reduce the sheerness of the fabric.

Depending on what is being manufactured, designers use several factories in different parts of the world. When production begins, skilled workers with different areas of specialization—stretch fabrics, knitted goods, hand embroidery, suedes and leathers, silk shirts, fine coats and suits—undertake particular areas of the line.

Fashion merchandise moves directly from the manufacturer's point of production to the retailer. To promote sales, a designer will arrange for prompt deliveries, make appearances in stores to publicize his newest fashions, share the cost of an ad with a store, or attend media-covered events to strengthen his image. And when large reorders pour in, a trium-

Bethann Hardison: "Stephen Burrows's clothes have a sense of humor. He isn't interested in going to publicity galas or putting on a black tie; he'd be happy doing designs and sketches."

Charles Suppon: "Ours was a difficult divorce. I was Calvin Klein's only assistant while his empire was being built. The best thing for an assistant is to be anonymous, give all the help he can. There's no point in saying, 'I did that jacket.' "

phant smile may cross his lips—but only momentarily. It is already time for new ideas to take shape.

For success in the fashion industry expert financial management is as vital as creative resources. Without it a designer is condemned to making the equivalent of home movies rather than Hollywood productions. A number of options are open to an ambitious young designer as he struggles up the slippery ladder of success. For example, he can begin as an established designer's assistant. Clovis Ruffin worked for Giorgio Sant'Angelo, Fernando Sanchez for Yves St. Laurent, and Charles Suppon for Calvin Klein. Halston designed hats for Lily Daché, and Donna Karan, who was employed by Anne Klein, became chief designer after the latter's death. Or he can launch his own line with a business partner and eventually buy him out, as Bill Blass did, or maintain the liaison, as Calvin Klein has. The $12,000 Klein borrowed twelve years ago from Barry Schwartz, his close friend and business partner, has since been parlayed into a fashion empire based on ready-to-wear ($70 million in sales of men's wear, $30 million from women's wear, and $100 million from jeans), cosmetics, and intricate licensing agreements with mass merchandisers. "Part of my success is due to Barry's business expertise," Klein admitted to *W*. "There are lots of talented designers, but very few Barry Schwartzes."

Norma Kamali is one of the rare designers who controls all aspects of her business. Her spectacular limited-edition fashions appeal to trendsetters seeking a highly individualistic look. (According to clotheshorse and journalist Phyllis Tweel, "Norma makes you feel like a woman. She satisfies my dreams.") In 1968 Kamali owned a small dress shop on Fifty-third Street. When she couldn't find clothes exciting enough for her ever-growing clientele, she gave herself a crash course in fashion design. Her early creations included black-and-gold stretch Lurex pedal pushers and leather hot pants that Seventh Avenue manufacturers soon copied; she made couture clothes from parachutes and sleeping bags, jumpsuits in black stretch jersey, and the sexiest bathing suits in the world. Today the multitalented Kamali, who prizes her independence above all else, sells striking clothes to customers who praise her originality.

Daniela Morera: "There are few designers who really change shapes. Most do very little, and have become important because of the publicity created around them."

Manufacturing on a larger scale requires more money. If a designer yearns for the mass market, he must be able to buy fabric months in advance of production. Generally this means finding a backer (silent or otherwise) to provide the necessary funds. Some designers who attempted to mass-market their clothes themselves have discovered that Seventh Avenue is impossible for the inexperienced to negotiate. Stephen Burrows, the first major black American designer, started at Henri Bendel in the design studio run by his mentor, Pat Tennant. Three years later Burrows decided to set up his own company and "dress the world." Not long after his debut, however, stores were cutting their orders from $40,000 to $8,000 a year; poor business practices, as well as the difficulty factories were having in executing Burrows's famous zigzag stitching, kept his energetic clothes from being shipped on time. But the unusually talented Burrows proved to be lucky. Geraldine Stutz, president of Bendel's, and Pat Tennant invited him back. Today, Burrows's company is called "Stephen Burrows for Pat Tennant."

Halston was provided with the most sophisticated marketing apparatus available when Norton Simon, Inc., a $1.8 billion corporation, paid him $10 million for his business and his name. In return the company gets a five-percent royalty on every sale of a product bearing Halston's stamp; and Halston designs everything from ready-to-wear that sells from $50 to $2,500, to uniforms for the U.S. Olympic Team, Braniff Airways, and the New York City Police Department, to custom-made evening gowns. As a result of Halston's talent and consistently high taste, both his and Norton Simon's fortunes have skyrocketed to the tune of $100 million per year.

Certain backers provide only money; others are entrepreneurs who will run a designer's business for a percentage of the profits. Ben Shaw, one of Seventh Avenue's more innovative backers, can help put together the entire production. Shaw's skill lies in combining teams of powerful designers, equally talented production managers, and aggressive sales managers who run the showrooms. Although contracts vary, each of Shaw's designers receives a salary, a percentage of sales, and special bonuses throughout the year.

Stewart Kreisler, a thirty-year-old whiz kid representing the new Seventh Avenue, was an undisputed although short-lived leader in this sort of

Stephen Burrows creating the windows that show his fashions at Bendel's.

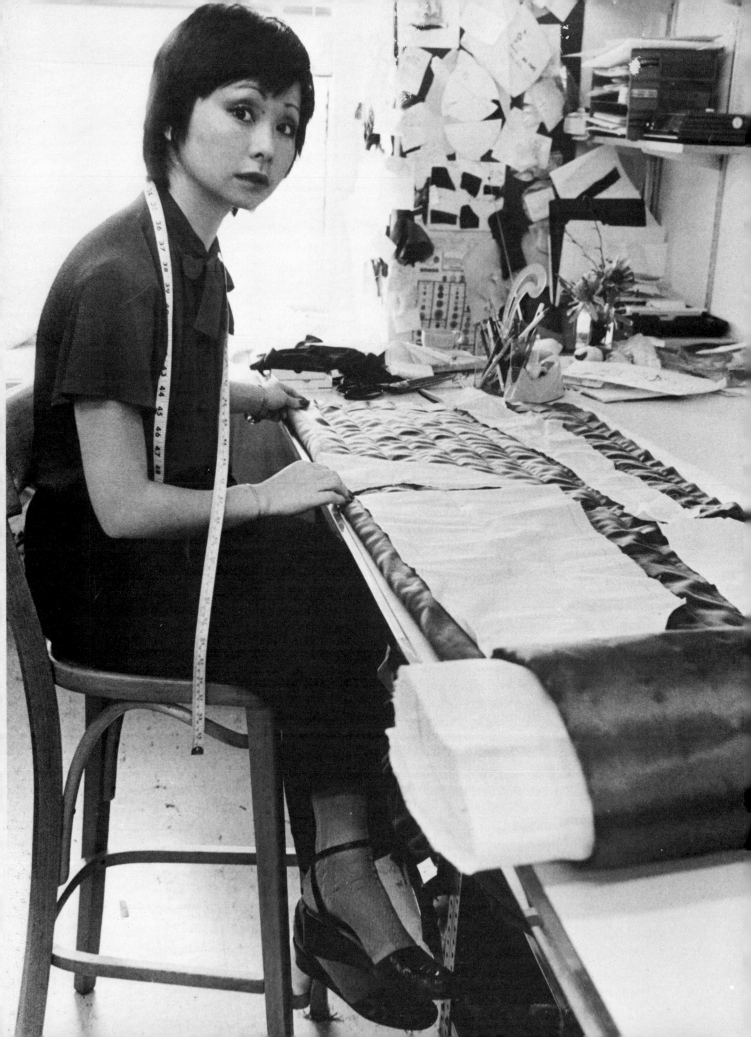

Daniela Morera: "Without inventing anything, Calvin Klein has become successful; I admire the fact that he's dressed so many women . . . Many of the truly creative designers never make any money."

backing. Although Kreisler rarely received personal press coverage, his seven-year-old business, the Kreisler Group, had made him a multimillionaire with an eighty-acre estate in Connecticut, and the respect of an industry that thrives on gossip. But suddenly in the summer of 1979 it was revealed that the Kreisler Group was in debt for $8 million—despite the phenomenal success of the Ralph Lauren women's wear collection that he backed. Designers who had been under his umbrella have moved on to find new financial backing, perhaps illustrating all too graphically the quixotic nature of this business.

Even when there is the right combination of talent, instinct, and backing, success cannot be insured. As both new and established designers realize, fashion is very much a personality business in which the creator is sold along with the creations. Personal appearances have become invaluable marketing tools. Through meeting with the public in stores, a designer can discover who his potential customer is and what she or he wants. This makes it possible to cast his new ideas in a marketable mold; at the same time shoppers can learn how to accessorize new looks through fashion shows and slide presentations.

Whereas only five or six years ago most customers were unaware of whose label they were wearing, today the same people are acutely conscious of designer names. This awareness is carefully reinforced by the appearance in stores of an immaculately attired Bill Blass; a self-assured Princess Diane Von Furstenberg; a model-slim Donna Karan (herself on the best-dressed list); a charming, boyish Calvin Klein; an irrepressible Carol Horn; and ivory-skinned Mary McFadden, who traveled to thirty cities last year with her quilted coats, classic gowns, and unique jewelry; an indefatigable Willie Smith; or a debonair Oscar de la Renta, whose name appears on no fewer than fifty-five products.

In a period when fashion is big business, when people think and care about what they wear and attempt to project an image that is aesthetically

Bill Kaiserman: "In most cases, if I see something overly feminine and frilly, it was probably designed by a homosexual."

Behind the scenes: one of the assistants at Regina Kravitz's design studio.

Ralph Lauren: "I respect Halston for building his own industry. I respect someone who creates his own identity."

pleasing, designers are being treated like movie stars; as Karl Lagerfeld noted, "It can become dangerous if one believes all the compliments." They have become full-fledged celebrities. Their names are stamped on countless products; they are given awards, paid homage to; fashion ladies seek invitations to their homes. They are stars—shooting stars who either ride high and maintain their speed or drop unceremoniously out of sight. They are radiant bodies who challenge our visual perceptions as they soar across a sequined sky.

In the past mammoth Hollywood movie studios were the sole creators of stars. No one anticipated that the behind-the-scenes designer would emerge front and center, amassing fortunes and fans. Many have attracted a cadre of "fashion groupies." Admittedly these women are a more sophisticated breed than their rock-culture counterparts, but nevertheless they admire a designer enough to follow his dictates and wear his clothes season after season. Lauren Hutton, Nancy Reagan, and Liv Ullmann are often seen wearing Calvin Klein; Bianca Jagger, Lauren Bacall, and Jackie Onassis choose Halston; Diane Keaton adores Ralph Lauren; Nancy Kissinger and Eileen Ford wear Bill Blass; and Lena Horne and Monique Van Vooren are among Sant'Angelo's celebrity clients.

Press coverage extends far beyond their customers, however, and into the designers' private lives. Elegant Oscar de la Renta and his charming wife, Françoise, are photographed redecorating their Connecticut home. World-traveler Egon Von Furstenberg is shown escorting a well-known beauty to a spectacular country wedding in France. The usually imperial Halston hosts a private drag party for Studio 54 employees, and Betsey Johnson lunches on the roof of her three-thousand square-foot pink SoHo loft with her current beau and her delightful daughter Lulu. Self-confident Bill Blass strolls along Seventh Avenue with one of his jet-set clients, while a perpetually tan Sant'Angelo emerges from Xenon with a gorgeous almond-eyed model on either arm; and Diane Von Furstenberg, who made herself more important than her clothes, is caught taking a sixty-second dance break at Studio 54.

Anonymous: "Calvin's timing is his genius. He knows when women are ready to be layered to death or pared down."

Bill Kaiserman: "I had tantrums when I realized people were copying me."

Some designers insist on privacy and never mix business with pleasure, no matter how many new customers they could acquire through a sparkling social life. An outspoken Giorgio Sant'Angelo "won't sit at boring dinners or play bridge with society ladies who don't deserve to be society ladies." Geoffrey Beene is a legend along Seventh Avenue for the things he doesn't do. *Vogue* described him as, "A man who values his work and his privacy beyond all else . . . He doesn't have big splashy showings with celebrities and photographers. He doesn't appear on talk shows or go to department stores to tell women with fat hips that they would look good in brown. Most of the time, he won't even tell writers what fashionable women he dresses; they include Jacqueline Onassis. He does not have a PR person or an advertising director." Donna Karan is another designer who feels that, "Communication to the public is through our clothes, not our personalities . . . Fashion is a glamorous business; each designer has to decide how much time to devote to socializing."

Calvin Klein admits, "I enjoy the idea of being anonymous sometimes. I like to go to Studio 54, dance, and not have to talk about fashion." Because of his fame Klein was forced to pay $100,000 in cash for the release of his kidnapped daughter. Before he took refuge from a relentless press, he told a *Newsweek* reporter, "I just never considered myself a celebrity."

Although Halston is constantly invited out by clients, he rarely mingles with them. Instead he socializes with a tightly knit group that may occasionally include a client like Liza Minnelli (who received a list of exactly what to wear, with what, when he began dressing her). When Liza went to Rio, *WWD* reported that she brought Halston's entire resort collection, including umbrellas because she wanted to avoid the sun.

Other designers welcome invitations and squire socially prominent fashion ladies whose investments in designer collections are noteworthy. Attendance at dinner parties and charity balls ensures extensive press coverage for the designer and invaluable contact with an endless assortment of women who measure their status by their ability to buy new

Egon Von Furstenberg (told *WWD*): "Diane Von Furstenberg is a better business person than I. She pinpointed a need. What I would have done would have been frills and feathers."

Bernie Ozer: "Stephen Burrows understands that *Ain't Misbehavin'* woman like no other."

clothes at frequent intervals. As Halston has remarked countless times, "You're as good as the people you dress."

In addition to creating their own collections, a number of designers have acquired empires of previously unheard-of dimensions through countless licensing agreements. A couture line is a loss leader generating great prestige but little profit; under licensing franchises, mass manufacturers of cars, perfume, sunglasses, furniture, and jeans (the hottest designer-name category) pay a designer—generously—for his or her magical name. In the 1970s, when Seventh Avenue became a pacesetter in areas other than clothing, licensing turned designers into brand names. As a *WWD* photographer remarked, "Designers can't think of enough new ways to make money."

At the Anne Klein studio Donna Karan and Louis Dell'Olio supervise some fifteen designers who work on everything from bed linens to scents for manufacturers licensed to use the company's name.

"If an item is made in a special color and fabric and the end result is something more fashionable," Bill Kaiserman feels that "a higher price is justifiable."

Of course there are designers who simply sell their names to manufacturers and have little involvement with the products. As one fashion-world habitué asked, "How can a top designer hang out in a disco until 5:00 A.M. and not sacrifice quality control?" Whatever its quality, merchandise bearing a designer's name gives customers a sense of status even if they cannot afford a Geoffrey Beene coat, Bill Blass beaded gown, or Fendi purple fox jacket. As Jamie Wolf points out in a perceptive *Harper's* magazine piece, "Labels provide a kind of warranty, however fragile or meretricious, a feeling of certification, an ineffable reassurance." Although designers derive the bulk of their profits from licensing, customers benefit from such agreements only when the designer actually oversees the operation and contributes a concept that reflects his artistic point of view. If a designer simply sells his name for status and income, the result will be an indifferent product or an out-and-out rip-off; on the other hand, if he cares about the products that bear his name, merchandise can be enhanced. A repetitive line of belts or scarves season after season is fair warning that a designer's name is meaningless—a customer would be far better off purchasing a product of similar quality at lower cost.

Bill Kaiserman with laudatory flowers after his stunning show.

Zandra Rhodes (told *Newsweek*): "Halston could sell the emperor's new clothes; he has a gift for putting things over, and that's not a criticism. You can design the best clothes in the world, but if you can't sell them, what's the point."

An even more recent trend involves American designers offering clothes priced lower than their Seventh Avenue or couture lines—either through new licensees or divisions of their own companies. Julio is doing Daydreams; John Anthony is selling John Anthony, Pret; Halston, who obviously likes the idea of moving from snob to mass appeal, is designing in every category. As Pat Tennant described Stephen Burrows's new endeavor to *Vogue,* "In the couture collection a top may retail for $200; in The Silk Fashion Group, it's $50 to $80, which makes it more affordable to more women." Besides boosting sales, such agreements encourage experimentation in new areas. Synthetic fabrics may be used in place of natural ones, or material will be ordered from the Orient instead of specialized European firms. Generally the less expensive line is introduced a season later to avoid reducing the effect of the primary collection.

Whether designers sell expensive originals or more of what they do best at lower prices, they provide the much needed possibilities of change and visual excitement to daily life. By constantly rearranging color, shape, and proportion, they enable a customer to repackage her body and consider herself an ever-changing living sculpture.

Just as the extraordinary Chanel established her reputation through a simple, skillfully tailored, collarless suit, many contemporary designers have become identified with particular looks. Calvin Klein makes low-keyed clothes from luscious fabrics (charmeuse satin, suede, handkerchief linen) that epitomize quality. Halston is responsible for a pared-down, zipperless, buttonless elegance, for reviving the one-shoulder dress and the shirtwaist, and for transforming the unexciting caftan into high fashion. Perry Ellis creates lived-in, slouchy, witty, everyday clothes. Blass is known for his expert tailoring and carefully composed look; Burrows, for sensuous clothes dramatized by electric color combinations, zigzag stitching, and "lettucing" (a term for curved edges coined by the ubiquitous Diana Vreeland); Julio, for a one-size-fits-all, luxurious evening look featuring kimonos, bubble tops, and narrow pants; Sant'Angelo, for layered gypsy dressing, bodywear, an updated American Indian look complete with feather ornaments in the hair. Ralph Lauren is noted for the Gatsby

Perry Ellis at his design studio.

and English looks as well as western styles epitomized by flounced prairie skirts, shearling vests, fringed buckskin jackets. Oscar de la Renta creates opulent, glittery evening clothes. Mary McFadden makes seductive hand-painted coats and fluid pleated dresses that wrap the body in bias cuts. Willie Smith designs witty, wearable, reasonably priced sportswear in natural fibers, and Geoffrey Beene offers a European-flavored look featuring exquisitely detailed trimmings and closings. Donna Karan and Louis Dell'Olio's designs are chic and functional. Fernando Sanchez is famous for outstanding at-home wear that is sophisticated, sexy, and fun indoors or out; Carol Horn is known for her irreverent layering of jacket over jacket, vest over tunic, skirt over petticoat or pants.

Generally the press concentrates on a designer's work and accepts his facade of polished perfection. If reporters probed further, they would discover complex personalities that are by turns temperamental, energetic, charismatic, insecure, curious, vain, self-confident, childlike, perceptive, narcissistic, and self-disciplined. By harnessing all these characteristics and still others, designers create fashions that enable women to change their style, their mood, or their roles. Although designers are serious people in a serious business, they're always aware that, as Stephen Burrows says, "Fashion should be fun."

CHAPTER THREE

THE MODEL

A PRETTY FACE IS NOT ENOUGH

> "A good model is like a Thoroughbred
> horse, but a thoroughbred horse has
> got to have a good rider, and a good
> model has to have a good photographer."
> —A prominent fashion photographer

It's a common assumption that a successful model gets by on good looks, good bones, and the right height and weight. In fact that's just for starters. As she turns, undulates, glides, and vamps on a runway or before a camera, she must understand innately what any piece of clothing can and cannot do. Her megawatt smile cannot evaporate; rather she must sparkle more and more as a shooting continues, convincing everyone that she is the most beautiful woman in the world—and the most joyous. Like an actress in a silent film, she projects an indefinable aura that ultimately can catapult her into superstar status.

And a good model *is* an actress. She must be able to step into any situation and perform, projecting the appropriate expression and capturing the mood that will sell a particular product. With split-second timing she can change her look as she tilts her head, rearranges her posture, or executes an imperceptible turn. Suddenly she's become the woman who loves diamonds, delights in dashing through traffic, adores her image in an Art Deco mirror, fondles her companion's hair, flirts outrageously with a stranger at a seaside café, perches on a mountain peak, or basks beneath a tropical sun in a handkerchief-sized bikini.

To assume an attitude that presents a product most effectively, a model must put aside any personal problems, establish a rapport with the photographer, and create a calm inner environment amidst a chaotic set filled with nervous clients, stylists, and assistants. Like an actress, she summons memories and fantasies that evoke a perfect world in which the viewer longs to participate. Asked to project happiness, Lauren Hutton recollects a scuba-diving expedition; another model visualizes her latest lover; a third concentrates on an upcoming trip to Brazil where she may meet that photographer she worked with once and never forgot.

The frenetic preparations models
must undergo prior to a show.

Ellen Harth: "Being a model doesn't necessarily mean you always have good sense—her good sense may become clouded by money."

A model's survival depends on practicing the type of diplomacy found at high-level peace conferences. The high-strung, high-pressure fashion business has its share of people with elephantine egos. Some photographers explode at the slightest provocation and function best only after they have shattered the nerves of everyone around them; some tunnel-visioned art directors never take risks because of their perpetual state of anxiety about whether the results will match their clients' expectations. And, of course, the designers themselves must be appeased.

This balancing act requires creativity and concentration; the model is at all times the center of attention and the focus of universal concern. As Farrell Connor, a top Ford model for twenty-one years, told *The New York Times,* "Still photography is much more precise than TV or motion pictures, and you must be aware of the differences. You mustn't contrive or force anything, because the camera doesn't lie." And because the camera exposes its subject mercilessly, the model must be worthy of its scrutiny.

It is her metamorphosis into an exquisite hothouse flower blooming in the rarefied atmosphere of a photographer's studio that earns her from $500 to $1,000 a day. Clients know their money is well spent: it is the model's look that sells the product. Her irresistible combination of beauty and personality occasionally gleans her as much as $200,000 or more a year. Cheryl Tiegs, for example, owns a $450,000 mansion in Bel-Air, California.

But while some models exude as much glamour in real life as on the set, others are quite colorless without a camera to flirt with. It is their chameleon nature that sets them apart from ordinary mortals. Halston told *Harper's Bazaar,* "I know girls who are not pretty at all, but by the time they paint their faces and have their hair done, they look incredible." Ray Crespin, a free-lance fashion director for *Vogue,* remembers the first time she saw a particular model at a shoot: "I noticed a child with a plump face, curly red hair, and no makeup. Within a short time she transformed herself into a raving beauty and began to use her body and facial expressions in an amazing way."

Nevertheless most models sport a perpetual aura of glamour that makes them trophies for the wealthy, high-powered men who relentlessly pursue them. Cultivated by a small group of powerful people who collect the young, beautiful, and successful (and abandon them when they no

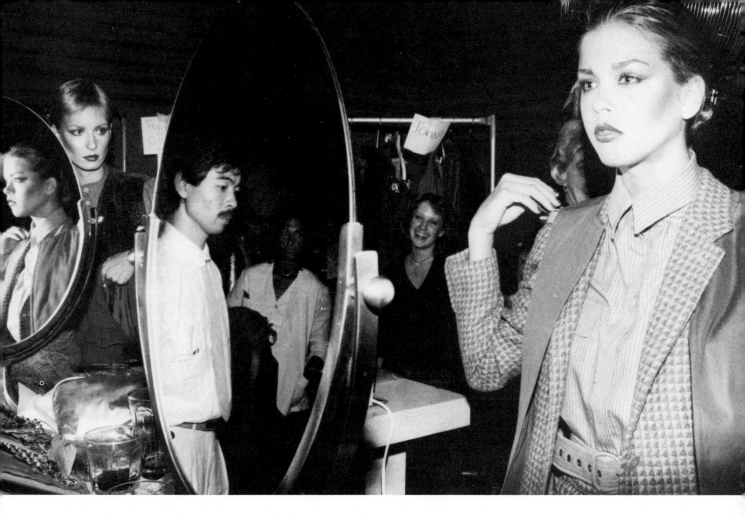

longer fit that description), cover girls are invited to and accept only "A-list" party invitations. They vacation on private island retreats whenever there is a short break in a tight work schedule, wear clothes given to them or bought at wholesale prices that rival those of the "beautiful people," travel all over the world from Morocco to Mozambique. Top models are inundated with images of themselves peering from billboards, television sets, and magazines.

Like designers, models are today's stars. Their private lives and their escorts are duly chronicled in gossip columns. They expect and usually get preferential treatment wherever they go, and they are envied by those who lead less glamorous lives. Appolonia, an exuberant six-foot beauty with a china-doll face, told *Viva* magazine that "the lure of a love affair and reggae would make me fly to Jamaica every weekend." The journalist noted that, "Apple's dining companions are the likes of Mick Jagger when

Ellen Harth: "Being beautiful doesn't mean that models are secure; at times friends or people in their lives influence their decisions. For instance—moving from one agency to another."

A prominent fashion photographer: "A female model is different every day; men's fashion is forced; the only new thing is the scruffy look."

---

he's in town. Her friends are Andy Warhol's clique and movie producer Bob Evans's circuit; Sam Spiegel and Jack Nicholson are ringside fight companions." *Viva* reported that when Appolonia was questioned about a reservation at One Fifth Avenue, a Greenwich Village restaurant that prides itself on its elegant atmosphere, she replied in French, "No, I don't have one, and I'm sure it's not necessary."

"It must be nice to be sure," observed the maître d'.

Models who have achieved star status often rely on a mentor for advice concerning their personal style, their relationships, and their careers. This friend or lover may introduce them to people who can make them richer or still more famous. Headstrong Appolonia credits Ara Gallant, wizard hairdresser-turned-photographer, as the greatest influence in her life. He gave her the look she loves via a spectacular hairstyle and new makeup, photographed her, helped decorate her apartment, found a designer to make her magnificent clothes, and introduced her to powerful magazine editors. And Margaux Hemingway's career was managed so brilliantly by her man-about-town ex-husband, Errol Wetson, that she evolved from an unpolished diamond into a supermodel complete with a million-dollar contract from Fabergé.

But with or without a mentor it isn't easy to reach that level—and it's even more difficult to stay there. It's not quite true that a model's life is an extravagant carousel ride with tinkling music and a gold ring always in sight. Behind the mannequin's smiling face and easy manner is a moody, often lonely person who craves constant attention. Even those born beautiful must work to look beautiful at all times. Says Ingo, a top international male model, "It's not models who are opportunists—it's the entire fashion world that wants you to be the most attractive and the most charming. They want your soul, and it's impossible to give that. Selling yourself to different clients five or six times daily without becoming hardened is very difficult."

Matt Collins, a male model who earns $1,000 per day, told *Interview* magazine, "It's such an insecure business. There aren't that many men's products. The big panic is that I won't work tomorrow." Moreover male models are relentlessly pursued by people of both sexes who consider them extravagant decorations that light up a room with their good looks.

Waiting to begin the fashion show.

A prominent fashion photographer: "Models are into contracts and star billing today. Some of them get very bitchy; as they get more famous, they say, 'I don't want to be photographed by X.'"

Like their female counterparts they develop a cynical attitude; they're aware they have more to offer than toned bodies, sculpted faces, and mysterious eyes.

Models whose looks depart from the norm also have reason to worry. Exotic blacks and Hispanics complain that American clients won't use them on covers because they don't conform to Middle America's classic, blond-haired, blue-eyed image. These models either play down their individualism or pursue careers in Europe where their unique appeal is appreciated. One black model recalls, "In the mid-sixties, when all the agencies wanted everyone to know that they had hired a black, I couldn't get work—I was considered too light-complected."

But whatever their color, background, or income many models exist on a surrealistic razor's edge; they are constantly aware that their looks are fading a little every day and that younger, fresher versions of themselves are poised in the wings waiting for their moment to perform. The more realistic among them use modeling as a stepping-stone to other careers. Fashion design and fashion consulting are two possibilities. China Machado, for example, left modeling to become senior editor at *Harper's Bazaar,* then a designer in her own right, and is now a film stylist. Coty-Award-winning model Conrad Bell, who once fell off a runway during a fashion show and returned to the stage without missing a beat, is designing extravagant men's furs and rugged outerwear. He may be the first professional male model who successfully made the transition from wearing to designing clothes. Public relations was the next step for Sunny Griffin, director of beauty and fashion for Avon, who holds seminars and handles product publicity. Acting lured Ali MacGraw, Charlotte Rampling, Candice Bergen, Elsa Martinelli, Lauren Bacall, Margaux Hemingway, and Lauren Hutton. And Ellen Harth and Wilhelmina established model agencies of their own. When Wilhelmina decided that she could model in her sleep, she knew she had finished her last assignment—even though no one else *sensed* it.

Most female models' careers last ten years. There are exceptions; Cheryl Tiegs, whose annual income is estimated at $300,000, and Lauren Hutton, who has a $500,000 contract with Revlon, are both over thirty and still project a tremendous, highly saleable spontaneity.

Sensuous Appolonia being fitted for one of Bill Kaiserman's swimsuits and a jacket.

A prominent fashion photographer: "Lauren Hutton is scrubbed, sexy, intelligent, real—the way women should look now."

Success sometimes goes to a model's beautiful head. Inundated with praise for her looks, she may believe her own notices and neglect the development of more meaningful attributes. Some behave in ways that irritate their clients; a strong-willed personality occasionally interrupts the flow of a shoot by refusing to wear the makeup painstakingly applied by an experienced cosmetician. Such unprofessionalism may be overlooked once or twice, but eventually a model labeled "difficult" will begin to lose work.

Models at their peak are frequently confronted with the fantasies, expectations, and prejudices of others. Lauren Hutton told *Ambience* magazine, "I've met people who apparently felt that by virtue of being attractive, I was dumb. It's still a prevalent cliché. Unfortunately by being attractive, women can get what they want; they don't develop their personalities or sense of humor. But it's a stifling way to live. Who wants to just sit around and be vacuous? If someone is condescending to me because I'm attractive, it says more about their personality than mine." Those models without Hutton's insights may realize at thirty-five that their talents are limited to being beautiful, and the discovery that their skin-deep glamour is fading is painful to accept.

In the meantime lucrative and prestigious assignments make a model feel secure. But a modeling career is filled with rebuffs—there is always someone the client finds more personable, more graceful, more beautiful. A continuous round of rejections causes even a successful model to fear that it will be downhill from then on. One spectacular beauty voices a common complaint: "Sometimes I feel frightened and don't know what I'll do when I can't sell my looks anymore. Even though I'm accepted by the majority of clients I see, I take even one rejection personally." Some are realistic enough to say, "If I get the job, fine. If not, okay. Maybe the timing isn't right." Others can't deal with the anxiety of waiting two hours to see a potential client only to be told that they are not the right "type."

Repeated rejections cause many new models to drop out of the business within a year and motivate others to sign with European agencies in an attempt to get a fresh start. Although fees are lower in Europe (a top model in Paris makes $50,000 annually as opposed to $150,000 to $200,000 in America), and the working day is longer (photographers shoot until 10:00 P.M., with a two-hour lunch break sandwiched in), it is

Top print model Margrit Ramme, relaxing before a photography session.

A prominent fashion photographer: "Many clients prefer Barbie dolls that they can push around. The public is dying for heroines: first Farrah, now Cheryl Tiegs is being promoted. I prefer to work with hot, sexy, modern nineteen- and twenty-year-olds. I like Sexy Ladies. I don't like ladies."

easier to achieve superstar status; there are fewer models and more fashion magazines, such as *Elle, Marie-Claire;* Italian, British, and French *Vogue;* Italian *Bazaar, Queen,* and *Harper's.* Many models get their careers off the ground overseas because the European mentality is freer and the taste level is higher; photographers are not only more willing to work with unorthodox types but are more experimental in general. As one European agent explains, "It's very common for Americans to go to Europe where the photographers are; we do the work and send them back to the U.S. The American market is timid and would rather use a known quantity." After six months abroad some mannequins return to their original New York agency armed with a fabulous portfolio—and sometimes an exotic new name—or switch to another agency. Along with their endless anxiety models are chronically hopeful.

Although every prom queen may aspire to be a model, such dreams tend to evaporate in the real world. Out of the several thousand young women who walk in off the streets or are discovered by designers, editors, talent scouts, photographers, or agents on American and European scouting tours, only about fifteen are accepted annually by agencies—and only five last through the first year.

Every morning bright-smiling, dry-mouthed hopefuls assault the agencies. In the reception rooms they sit under the famous Irving Penn portrait of Eileen Ford surrounded by a dozen former top models or admire the *Vogue* covers of ex-model Wilhelmina Cooper. They visit the modern white offices of Johnny Casablancas, the East Sixties townhouse of Zoli, or the Stewart Agency, which was founded by Stewart Cowley. They wait to be appraised with the thoroughness that race-horse owners lavish on new acquisitions. If one of them seems to have the right looks, she is ushered into the offices of Eileen Ford, Wilhelmina, Johnny Casablancas, Zoli, or Stewart Cowley. There she is told, "You have potential." Or more

Wilhelmina: "The worst scandals concern models working in Europe."

Anonymous model: "I've never heard of any model advancing her career by sleeping with a photographer."

frequently, "Your eyes are too close together, your lips are too thin; your shoulders aren't broad enough; your legs are too heavy." In this tough, competitive business there isn't time to give anyone a break.

To have even a chance at success, young women require wide-set eyes, slender legs, healthy hair and skin. Depending on the category (juniors, misses, high fashion), they range from 5' 7" to 5' 11", weigh 105 to 120 pounds, have 33" to 34" busts, 22" to 24" waists, and 33" to 35" hips. In addition to being lean and lithe, they must project charisma—that special something—in front of a camera. Aside from looking handsome and decidedly masculine and weighing approximately 165 pounds, male models need broad shoulders, narrow hips, slim waists, and long, muscular legs. High-fashion magazines like *Vogue* favor elegant, chiseled, indifferent-looking males with sucked-in cheeks, while advertisers prefer all-American, bland types who appeal to a wide audience that might feel threatened by an overwhelmingly sexy man. In this country female models dominate fashion photography. In America, except in publications like *Gentlemen's Quarterly* (Condé Nast's first American men's fashion magazine), *The New York Times*'s seasonal men's fashion section, or *Playboy*, males usually serve as backdrops, with only their shoulders or hand being photographed.

Although agents insist they can always spot model material—that combination of physical beauty, magnetism, and poise—occasionally they make mistakes. Four agencies turned down Lauren Hutton, with her less-than-perfect features, before Eileen Ford, the doyenne of the modeling world, signed her—and nine months passed before Hutton got her first booking and began moving toward superstardom.

Not all models are under contract. But if an agency believes in her potential, a contract will be signed "to keep the model from running out the

Johnny Casablancas: "The public doesn't know the names of models who make two-hundred thousand dollars a year. There's a demystification of models today; the star system has virtually disappeared except for someone like Roseanne Vela [Ford model]. She's one of the last cases of acute 'staritis' that still works. Peter Max, her artist-boyfriend, even redoes the lights during a shoot."

Johnny Casablancas: "Modeling brings out a tendency towards narcissism."

door under criticism," explains Wilhelmina. The contract will be broken if she endangers an agency's reputation because she takes drugs, accepts and cancels bookings at the last minute, continuously arrives late, or is careless about her personal appearance (one top model used to arrive at her bookings with dirty fingernails and unkempt hair). And if her career doesn't take off, the agency may break the contract. Models have a slightly more difficult time severing legal connections. When Wilhelmina was granted an injunction to stop top model Iman (who resembles Egypt's Queen Nefertiti) from working for another agency, Iman announced that she was five months pregnant; by the time she had her baby, her contract had expired.

An agent will help a beginner choose her best portraits for the agency's "head sheet," which shows front views of all models and lists vital statistics and sometimes hourly and daily rates. The director or an assistant also helps prepare her composite or "calling card," a brochure with statistics and a variety of photos that reveal her different looks and moods. Composites can cost thousands of dollars, depending on their quality and whether they are printed in black and white or color, and are mailed to the hundreds of prospective clients who keep them on file.

To gather pictures for her portfolio and to get as much experience as possible working in front of a camera with many different photographers, a new model generally "tests" with a young photographer or assistant; this allows him to experiment and build his own portfolio as well.

During the first three months with the agency, modeling novices, no matter how attractive, undergo rigorous training in the use of makeup, posing in front of a camera, and behavior in a studio. They also receive a program of diet and exercise to incorporate into their daily routine (even the slimmest models have to worry about appearing overweight because the camera is merciless). They experiment endlessly to create the best mouth, the most perfect eyes, the most flattering hairstyle (and one that can be changed in five minutes). They practice holding a product gracefully, keeping a flashing smile from getting flat, and moving effortlessly in

Johnny Casablancas: "Models without a book, but with a look, should socialize."

Some of Halston's favorite runway models—here showing his evening gowns.

Johnny Casablancas: "Cheryl Tiegs [Ford] is a name beyond fashion. Models have to be careful about moving to personality modeling and doing limited things."

front of the camera. Some models endure extreme body renovation. Former agent Barbara Stone told the *New York Post* that Verushka, one of her clients, had one joint removed in each foot to make them smaller. "There you are on a set in gorgeous clothes, and no one can find shoes to fit your feet," Stone explained.

To earn its fifteen- or twenty-percent commission on a model's fees, the agency constantly updates the crucial portfolio, schedules bookings, circulates her pictures, and mediates between her and an employer if a problem arises (she may have gained weight or cut her hair without informing the prospective client). Because many models are from small towns and have led sheltered lives before arriving in New York City, an agent often dispenses advice. Newcomers are warned not to be extravagant in their first flush of success and not to work with certain clients no matter how personable they may seem (the names of well-known designers who live lavishly but forget to pay their bills are pinned above the bookers' desks as a daily reminder).

Establishing a good rapport with a booker is essential because it is she who is on the phone with clients, she who suggests which models to use. Each time a booker gets a request for an ivory-skinned, seventeen- to twenty-year-old, 5' 8" green-eyed blond, she'll send a troupe of models who fit the description to the client's office to determine which one is most suitable to sell the product.

Because she's constantly being sent on these "go-sees"—at least eighty per month—every model calls the agency several times a day to learn about her next appointments. Unless she's a superstar and can afford to refuse work, a model on vacation always notifies her booker of her whereabouts; clients tend to be fickle and forget anyone who's unavailable more than twice—even if she's ill or working abroad.

A model can be sent almost anywhere, for almost anything. A reasonably versatile type does frequent runway modeling. Editorial work, the

Pat Cleveland (top international runway model): "I've been a model for fourteen years, and every time I do photography or a show, it feels like the first time."

least lucrative but most glamorous, is an important showcase; clients often look in fashion magazines for a distinctive face. Advertising, especially cosmetic ads and mail-order catalogs, offers high fees to fashion models. But the most lucrative area is television. After joining either or both AFTRA (American Federation of Television and Radio Artists) or SAG (Screen Actors Guild), a model can earn $1,000 a day plus residuals each time a commercial is aired; one day's efforts can amount to $15,000 in overall fees.

Location work is exciting, romantic—and potentially a great deal of trouble. Though things occasionally go wrong, and unexpected bad weather can cost days and thousands of dollars, a model must appear overwhelmingly cheerful even when forced to spend hours standing on a hot pavement in a fur coat and the wrong-sized shoes. She must be prepared to jump again and again into an icy sea or endure a backache from re-

Jean Pagliuso (photographer): "My favorite models are sexy, understand their own bodies, and have a sense of humor."

maining immobile in a weighted skirt while she's pricked by pins and stylists constantly readjust her hair and makeup. She must cope calmly with food poisoning or bad news, boredom or the lack of adequate instructions. And she must forgo a tan on a tropical island in order to maintain a constant skin tone.

With reason, insurance companies regard models as an unstable, high-risk group. One of Helmut Newton's models developed an infection from sand imbedded in the wound where an ankle strap cut into her skin. Another model was asked to jog and simultaneously smile at the photographer; the result was a broken leg and a month in a cast without compensation. And recently one international model was forced to stop working temporarily because of vision problems that developed from the constant exposure to photographers' strobe lights. There are emotional problems as well. It is rare for a model to bring family members on location. One who did was so unmercifully teased by the indignant photographer that she and her family decamped in the middle of the night. The next morning ribbons of the film that held her image were found floating in the swimming pool.

Another model, having completed an assignment in Greece, was frustrated in her attempts to reach her next job in Italy by a severe storm. After ten anxiety-filled hours at the airport she shouted, "You must get me out! I'm on business!" Soon she was flying through the storm in a small private plane. When she realized there wasn't even a copilot, she stopped and asked herself, "Just what am I risking for my career?"

While a print model acts essentially with her face, a runway model must move with pantherlike grace and enough flair to hold the attention of an audience ranging from several hundred to a few thousand when she does a show in Europe or Japan. The models must be young enough to carry the latest fashions but mature enough to convince buyers that older women also will look attractive in them. These attenuated figures move through space with unfailing assurance. (Occasionally male models look thoroughly embarrassed on the runway, but their awkwardness is disap-

Jean Pagliuso (photographer): "I'm interested in models who have my own interests—who aspire to be liked or loved."

Wilhelmina model Cathy Belinger, showing one of Krizia's stunning evening creations.

Bethann Hardison: "Pat Cleveland moves like no other—with her long legs and marvelous wide-set eyes."

pearing as designers create high-fashion men's clothes and present them in extravagant productions.) Like trained actors the best runway models change character to fit the mood of the clothes. During a fashion show, in faster-than-the-speed-of-light changes, ultrachic types may soften their makeup, attach braids to their hair, and become blushing school girls who skip down the runway; later they make drop-dead entrances as sophisticates.

Although today's models do both live and photographic work, height requirements are stricter for fashion shows. Runway models tend to be taller and have broader shoulders and flatter hips and bosoms than those who do print work. (Occasionally a model's presence is so magnetic that she appears taller than she actually is.) Moreover a runway model lasts longer than a print model. As Wilhelmina, owner of one of New York's prestigious model agencies, explains, "If you're good as a coat hanger, there's no reason why a few wrinkles will keep you out of the business. An audience gets a quick image of a model and doesn't see every inch of her, as does the critical eye of a camera."

It was not until the 1970s that models regularly crossed categories. In the past two years, after rates were equalized by Ellen Harth, owner of the Ellen Harth Runway Model Agency, a number of successful print models became more than willing to be runway stars. Designer Calvin Klein prefers top print models such as Patti Hansen and Lisa Taylor for his shows; otherwise he'd have to rely on the veterans who appear at most of the shows during market week. "If you use pure runway models who are seen in many shows," he explains, "it gets a little boring." Runway models also have moved into print, especially after designers began to appreciate how well they look and move in clothes—and how they would enhance an ad.

A small group of models who never appear in fashion shows or advertisements supply the garment center with the perfectly proportioned bodies needed to make patterns ranging from junior sizes to a woman's size sixteen and a half. They earn $35 to $50 an hour instead of $75 to $125 because their faces are far less in demand than their figures.

Some faces are perfectly in tune with the times. A cursory glance at any fashion magazine or a quick flick of the TV dial reveals the image that advertisers adore: a natural, earthy, sexy beauty whose hair is windblown (courtesy of wind machines) and whose gaze is direct, who seems young

Carla Araque—her sexy and dramatic looks keep her in demand for showings.

Eileen Ford: "I'm a creator of models. Could I be prouder of Shelly [Smith] than I am of Roseanne [Vela]?"

and full of life. Just as fashion changes, so does the concept of beauty; each decade produces a new ideal that every young girl wants to emulate, a face that is seen on every cover, in every ad—until someone else comes along to be crowned the new top model by the press.

In the 1950s models smiled mysteriously and kept their private lives private. They were seldom known to their audience, which was far more interested in the clothes they wore than the lives they led. Later extraordinary-looking foreign models, attracted by the large fees paid by American clients, invaded America. The more memorable faces of the permissive 1960s—when fashion photography thrived on experimentation and thousands of dollars were lavished on producing spectacular pictures—included pouty, perfect-featured Jean Shrimpton, who was discovered by English superphotographer David Bailey, and the huge-eyed, sexless Twiggy, whose creator, Justin de Villeneuve, carried the art of career making to its zenith. The chameleonlike, 6' 1" tall, lion-maned Verushka was discovered by Diana Vreeland, whose perceptions are deemed infallible by the cognoscenti.

While this trio became the superstars of the decade, Dutch-born Wilhelmina, who appeared on more *Vogue* covers than any model in history, and earned more money, was known only by her face—never by name. Wilhelmina wasn't interested in a jet-set life or a publicist to promote her career. She remembers the 1960s as a period when, "No one realized that a high-fashion model could speak, because the look at that time was an untouchable, unreal, statuesque kind of appearance . . . No one knew exactly what modeling was about."

Today's top models may be celebrities, but only a handful have eccentric, strongly individualistic looks; Jerry Hall, Appolonia, and Pat Cleveland are among them. Most of the current cover girls—Roseanne Vela, Patti Hansen, Christie Brinkley, Lisa Taylor, and Cheryl Tiegs—are all-American, scrubbed, and smiling. Radiantly healthy, as approachable as the girl next door, they look as if they've just jogged for miles. All of them lack that ethereal aura popular in the '60s, which Diana Vreeland found far more interesting than the naturalism now prevalent. "There's too much blowing in the wind," the grande dame of fashion told *Newsweek.* "At one time it was fashionable to be made up, and it was not fashionable to have your clothes always falling off you and your hair falling down. A model becomes what today is, and what today is is the inner force of fashion. There is a certain monotony about the girls of today. It must be planned that way."

Eagle-eyed Eileen Ford, who has run a model agency for the last thirty-two years, agrees that, "Today's modeling business doesn't have the strong personalities that existed in the past, so that anyone who's at all different is regarded as really outstanding." Ford has a knack for finding those outstanding faces whom advertising and editorial people want most: stars like Karen Graham, Rene Russo, Roseanne Vela, and Lauren Hutton. Eileen and her husband Jerry are largely responsible for the professionalism and huge fees now standard in the industry. Models do not belong to a union; their rates have been raised to $75 to $150 per hour through the considerable efforts of the Fords. The couple also negotiated the first restrictive and highly lucrative contracts between their models and top cosmetic companies, thereby creating a new category: image girls whose faces endorse a product in the public mind. For example, Cheryl Tiegs represents Cover Girl and Virginia Slims throughout the world, Karen Graham has an exclusive contract with Estée Lauder; and Margaux Hemingway, the highest-paid model in history, works for Fabergé.

Eileen Ford observes that, "Modeling's a no-nonsense, no-excuse business, and a girl must be willing to devote her life to it. Models today are really dead serious about their work. The girl twenty or thirty years ago had a different mentality. She saw herself as a glamorous woman. It's hard to find models who think that way today—business is on their mind. There's a lot at stake, and the dollars are big."

After seven years at the top of her profession, former Ford model Wilhelmina and her husband, Bruce Cooper, established Wilhelmina Agency, Inc. in 1967. Wilhelmina, who discovered Elsa Peretti, Beverly Johnson, and Margaux Hemingway, feels qualified to give models the best advice, "since I know exactly what it's like to be used as a piece of flesh. Who can handle this business better than I? I really know the nitty gritty."

Zoltan Rendessy's eight-year-old Zoli Models is well known for an unusual, exotic, "personality" model.

Until 1977, the New York modeling world was controlled by Ford,

---

Eileen Ford (on Lauren Hutton): "She always seems spontaneous; when I first met her, she had an allure as a human being. I believe talent is there or it isn't."

Ray Crespin: "It's a mistake to turn young girls into stars; they're rattled by it, become difficult, and can't cope with adoration."

Wilhelmina, Zoli, and Stewart Cowley. The agencies competed fiercely but didn't quite entice models away from one another. Then along came continent-hopping thirty-six-year-old Johnny Casablancas. Head of the leading model agency in Europe, this Johnny-come-lately soon claimed a large share—approximately $5 million in 1978—of a business that's estimated at $30 million in New York alone.

Casablancas maintains a select stable of models who do advertising, editorial, catalog, and television work. His rapid success in a tightly controlled industry is due to his strong business background, close contact with photographers both in Europe and New York who prefer his easygoing manner, and models who enjoy the personal attention his bookers can provide because they have fewer models to work with.

Casablancas entered the business by falling in love with a young Parisian model who felt her agency wasn't doing a good job. To help her as well as himself, he established an agency that soon offered the cream of the talent, a process that he repeated in New York when he opened an office a few blocks from Eileen Ford's. An articulate, self-confident man, Casablancas denies the body-snatching techniques of which he's accused and professes not to understand why models should not move from one agency to another. "If the agent is doing a good job, the models won't leave," he states.

Whatever their reasons, models do leave. One hundred models earn over $50,000 a year; some twenty models earn $200,000. When top money-makers like Iman, Beverly Johnson, and Janice Dickenson (who has made $20,000 filming one commercial during a week in Japan) left the established agencies to sign with Casablancas, Ford and Wilhelmina lost a significant sum in commissions. They retaliated by suing Casablancas for $11.5 million—(the suit is still pending) in what became known in the industry as the "model wars."

Models' reactions to the uproar are not surprising; they consider the intense competition among the agencies a welcome change. As one remarked, "It's the first time that models are in a position to choose the agency that we want and get better contracts. It's a revolution that has made us more independent."

While models may welcome more say in their choice of agencies, their success still depends to a great degree on their own resourcefulness and

An ecstatic Billie Blair after an exhausting photographic session.

Wilhelmina: "The worst thing a model can do is let a client know that she doesn't give a damn."

hard work, as a look at a typical day-in-the-life of a top model reveals. Toukie Smith, who has been with Wilhelmina for the last three years, is a vibrant, ambitious woman who does ingenue as well as high-fashion photography. As a runway and photo model Toukie is in demand in Europe and Japan; she crosses back and forth between modeling worlds as frequently as businessmen cross town to conduct their affairs. This morning, she awakens at 6:30 A.M. to prepare for a 9:00 A.M. photo booking. After yoga exercises, a bath, and a healthy breakfast of yogurt, juice, whole-wheat bread, and vitamins, she packs her enormous tote bag with a magnifying mirror; curling iron; several pairs of panty hose; a strapless bra; a body stocking to flatten her breasts for a coed look; three pairs of shoes; a wide array of makeup and brushes for touch-ups or a full application in case there's no makeup stylist on the set; a head scarf to protect her hair when she changes garments; an emery board; a miniature sewing kit; facial tissues; comb; brush; Scotch tape for emergencies; appointment book; disco and classical cassettes and a small player to help her attain a suitable mood; a kimono to wear between takes; tea to calm her nerves.

Armed with the tote and her portfolio, she heads for her first appointment at a photographer's studio on Twentieth Street (many top photographers are located in this part of the city). When she's in her kimono, a hair stylist does her hair and a makeup expert spends forty-five minutes creating a glamorous face to set off the disco-oriented evening clothes she will wear. She slips on a sleek silk dress and stands still as the stylist tightens the back with a few pins.

Now Toukie steps on the seamless paper used as a backdrop and is handed a pair of sexy spike-heeled shoes. Under the glaring lights she responds to a blaring bossa nova beat and imagines the excitement of "attending a marvelous party with the most attractive man in town." She moves in and out of five or six standard poses, listens to directions from the photographer, and takes off. Her eyes flash; her expression becomes animated; she throws her head back. Smile. Click. Relax. The stylist wraps a silver-threaded scarf around the model's neck. Toukie shifts positions, undulating slowly to the rhythmic music. Smile. Click. Relax. Toukie leaves the set and changes into street clothes, while a second model steps onto the seamless paper and repeats the process.

With a half hour to get to her next appointment, Toukie is off and

Toukie Smith preparing to be photographed.

Ellen Harth: "A model has to go along with the look that the design-er wants from her, and she must be punctual; a designer certainly doesn't need any more aggravation before his show."

running. This time it's a "go-see" with a photographer who wants models who can disco roller skate. As the photographer looks through her portfolio, Toukie calls her booker to find out tomorrow's schedule and whether it is necessary to bring any special accessories. Then she races over to a New York City municipal swimming pool where she poses in bathing suits for the next two hours. Although it is mid-winter, she instantaneously evokes a balmy day as she struts to the edge of the diving board. Smile. Click. Relax. Toukie dresses in her street clothes and kisses the other models good-bye.

Next she brings Wilhelmina a batch of new slides from her latest assignment with top designer Issey Miyake in Tokyo (where a limo whizzed her from the airport to do three shows a day for a crowd of six thousand fashion fanatics). At the agency either Willy or an assistant help her choose the best shots to add to each of her portfolios on file in New York and Europe.

Next she devotes an hour to a manicure and pedicure, then heads for a private health club for a sauna and massage; in between she calls a photographer she worked with on some experimental shots to remind him to send her the pictures. Passing Bloomingdale's window as she taxis over to another photographer's studio for more test shots, she sees her image as a lifelike mannequin staring back at her. Finally she heads home.

Toukie eats before 6:00 P.M. because of the difficulty of shedding calories after late-night dinners. During the week she usually goes to bed by midnight because, "It's impossible to abuse my body with food, drink, or drugs and partying and be a successful model." She sighs and adds, "I work twenty-four hours a day."

Most top models do. Despite the hard work and incredible competition, modeling can be a fantastically rewarding field for those who combine good looks, discipline, personality, and perseverance. That is, if they do not succumb to their own beauty. Narcissus, as you may remember, did. Transfixed by his image in a limpid pool, he was ultimately transformed into a flower. And flowers are unlikely to be offered an exclusive contract.

CHAPTER FOUR

PUBLICITY BASHES AND THE GREAT CATALYST

THE PUBLICIST

"A publicist is like an alchemist who puts
the whole package together for her client."

—Roz Rubenstein

Fashion needs things to do and places to go. Fortunately there is always an occasion to promote somebody or something: a new perfume, a department store's decorator rooms, a boutique, a birthday, a ballet. Although some people prefer to consider fashion a branch of aesthetics, the more realistic know that it is a commercial venture—and a publicity bash is the perfect image-building and profit-making vehicle.

The publicist, who controls an event as a ringmaster controls a circus, is happiest when she has an appropriate occasion on hand. One of New York's greatest assets is an astonishing assortment of fashion and social celebrities who love to dress up and go out; it is the publicist's responsibility to plan a party that will attract the media along with enough chic, amusing, and wealthy guests. Those invited invariably include well-known personalities; American and multinational socialites; those acclaimed in their professions (plastic surgeons usually enjoy publicity, while doctors aligned with conservative hospitals shun it); impeccably mannered, slightly jaded, fine-boned young playboys and playgirls; a sprinkling of merchandisers; and the usual stargazers who can be counted on to worship the illuminati. For a charity benefit, enlisting celebrities to serve on a committee guarantees the attendance of several hundred top-flight guests.

Publicist Bobby Zarem, who celebrated the premiere of the film *Tommy* in a New York subway station, knows whom to invite to what. "The prince of publicity" told *The New York Times* that he would ask "Geraldine Stutz, Diana Vreeland, D.D. Ryan, Pat Kennedy, Jacqueline Onassis, Bianca Jagger, Diane Von Furstenberg, and Delfina Ratazzi anywhere, because they are sympathetic." These women are also charming, socially prominent, and the kind of guest who makes any event more prestigious. Most important they draw press coverage; the right people wearing the right design-

A party in honor of Erté's artistic efforts; this outfit is a Bill Cunningham creation.

ers' clothes generate mutually beneficial publicity in what can be
regarded as an ideal symbiotic relationship.

Although there is no master guest list that every publicist consults, a
select group of photogenic fashion devotees are routinely invited to everything; in their lavish homes stacks of invitations are scattered like wild-
flowers, and although they may wait until the last minute to respond,
there is always enough room for them. They tend to travel en masse so
they can entertain one another if no new diversion is available. Like glittery moths around a flame the fashion pack appears and reappears at the
right parties each night—somehow, no matter how late the hour, managing to look better than anyone else.

To attract these sleek, slender libertines to an event, a publicist must
promise something bigger and better. Perhaps no single party in recent
fashion history matched the launching of Yves St. Laurent's new perfume,

Opium. Among the more amazing aspects of this $250,000 extravaganza is that St. Laurent's backer, Charles of the Ritz, is a subsidiary of E. R. Squibb & Sons, Inc., an old, conservative pharmaceutical concern. Although Squibb was not exactly pleased with St. Laurent's name for the product, the designer insisted on Opium or nothing. His twelve-page poem expressing his feelings about the perfume and evoking the opulence and exoticism of the Orient finally convinced Squibb that no connection with an illegal drug was implied. The fact that St. Laurent was able to use the name despite its illicit connotations exemplifies the tremendous power a single designer can exert.

The party celebrating the birth of Opium was engineered by Marina Schiano (referred to as Yvita St. Laurent), who runs St. Laurent's ready-to-wear collections in America, and Renny Reynolds, an East Side florist to the rich. For the occasion the *Peking,* an old Chinese junk anchored at the South Street Seaport, was turned into a floating fantasy complete with dozens of banners flying from the four masts, a serenely smiling thousand-pound Buddha, masses of white cattleya orchids flown in from Hawaii, a disco, mountains of extravagant cocktail tidbits catered by Glorious Food, thirty cases of Boulinger champagne (the designer's favorite), thirty cases of Pinot Chardonnay, and more. In preparation the organizers secured fireworks permits, rain tents, and six security guards. They purchased disco tapes, seven hundred fifty down-filled pillows, bamboo furniture, and thousands of dollars worth of lanterns, fans, trays, and baskets (many of which reportedly vanished at the end of the party).

Over five hundred hand-addressed invitations were imported from Paris and hand delivered to an assortment of the young and fashionable, old and social, and representatives of couture, stores, and the media; the managers of YSL's boutiques in New York, however, were accidentally overlooked.

Fashion and life-style reporters from newspapers and magazines covered the party. NBC, ABC, CBS, Metromedia, and the BBC sent camera crews to record some nine hundred guests making drop-dead entrances in costly evening clothes, parading under a three-hundred-foot-long canopy decorated with Chinese silk lanterns, rose petals strewn along their path. Seventh Avenue was well represented by Fernando Sanchez, Giorgio Sant'Angelo, the de la Rentas, Mary McFadden, Calvin Klein, Pauline Trigère, Diane Von Furstenberg, Zandra Rhodes, Michaele Vollbracht, Bill Blass, Stephen Burrows, Bill Kaiserman, and Halston, who created a sensation when he escorted Cher (in a transparent black dress) up the runway.

Throughout the evening Yves St. Laurent was guarded by a phalanx of gorgeous models wearing geishalike makeup and his splendid Oriental-style clothes. The party's high point was a twenty-minute fireworks' display that exploded from two barges on the East River to spell out YSL. Soon afterward the guests abandoned ship clutching their Opium samples, limoed up to Studio 54, and danced until dawn.

Although some participants described the party as elegant, extravagant, and ravishing, designer Mary McFadden told *WWD,* "I didn't see many friends, but there were a lot of photographers . . . There are two approaches with a party like that: either you can create excitement or you can open a product elegantly, and they obviously took the first approach." An even more cynical view was expressed in *New Times* magazine. "Exactly what are you getting for your $100 an ounce besides $5.00 worth of chemical components?" the writer asked. "A pipe dream of packaging and poetry . . . Opium fanciers will be glad to know, however, that the packaging is very expensive. The container is handmade and the tassels are handsewn."

Richard Furland, Squibb chairman and admirer of Yves St. Laurent, told the press, "As far as I'm concerned, this is a purely social occasion." Nevertheless the party accomplished the classic aims of a publicity bash: it was one of the most photographed and talked-about parties of 1978, and it allowed the host to realize his most extravagant fantasies.

The "extravagance," averaging out to about $300 per guest, appears to have been worthwhile; it made Opium an instant household word—at least in those households that matter. A single party (along with brilliant advertising and packaging) had skyrocketed Opium to a key spot in the lucrative, competitive perfume market. Bloomingdale's sold $1,000 worth within two hours, and customers from coast to coast were unwilling to spend another day without the heady fragrance.

Any successful publicity campaign demands inventiveness. Whatever its basis, a function must intrigue the press. A $250,000 expenditure is one way to attract attention; but designers who hold less elaborate parties can still get results if they have enough imagination. At a Betsey Johnson fashion show her specialty, futuristic bodywear, was shown on models and nonprofessionals performing intricate steps on roller skates. After the applause subsided, the event evolved into a frenetic disco party.

Other designers prefer to begin with low-keyed fashion shows, saving the theatrics until later. Fastidious Karl Lagerfeld held a Venetian ball at which some four thousand of his favorite friends, including Paloma Picasso (who made the international best-dressed list several months later), ap-

peared in extravagant costumes as courtesans, street musicians, and royalty. Kenzo celebrated his birthday at Le Palace, the Parisian answer to Studio 54. The invitations, wrapped in white silk tissue and tiny violet buds, requested that guests dress as the opposite sex. While most of the women wore smoking suits, the men tottered around on stiletto heels, exhausted themselves, and left before 3:00 A.M.

Rather than throw a party or hold a fashion show, businessman Maurice Bidermann invited a crowd of social types and business people to the opening night of the Bejart Ballet of the Twentieth Century. Although the evening cost some $63,000, he attracted attention to Bidermann Industries, an umbrella for Calvin Klein, Don Robbie, Jean Paul Germain, and YSL men's wear.

New York's Studio 54, formerly the CBS sound studio, is a publicist's delight—perfect for those who want instant (although fleeting) attention and for celebrities who yearn to get lost in a crowd. A private party celebrating a designer, rock star, or film maker takes place nearly every night. Hordes of gorgeous, slim-hipped men in butter-soft leather or custom-made tuxedoes and breathtakingly beautiful women clad in shimmering clothes step out of limos (rented or otherwise) and are briskly ushered into Studio's inner sanctum, while those who aren't beautiful or powerful enough ooh and aah the celebrities' Kleig-lighted arrival. A large, mirrored hall bathed in perpetual darkness leads to the dance floor, which can be elaborately decorated for theme parties; gigantic posters, molded ice vases, and aromatic trees are moved in for the evening—transforming "Studio" (as the regulars call it) into a tropical paradise, a farm, lush Indian gardens complete with doves and peacocks, the North Dakota woods, or an Italian outdoor café. The result is an ever-changing visual landscape. A curtain separates private parties from the onslaught of Studio's members. As the evening progresses, the curtain is raised, and the haves and the would-haves share the same dance space.

In a timeless ambience of wall-to-wall people, the fantastically dressed guests create their own spectacle. Supple-bodied narcissists flash by in detached splendor; Felliniesque figures weave in and out of a crowd of ecstatic dancers and mesmerized observers. Posturing bartenders and chorus-boy waiters in boxer shorts serve drinks in time to the incessant beat. A tightly muscled man in a leopard mask, a clothespin clinging to his left nipple, watches his image in the smoky mirror. A charming Southerner skates by in a flounced chiffon dress, a straw hat perched precariously on top of a curly wig, hugging and kissing his many admirers. A would-be actress in a rainbow leotard, eyes outlined in blue sequins, headdress a mass of peacock feathers, dances by herself hour after hour. Visiting celebrities are ensconced on silver vinyl banquettes on a raised platform under the relentless eyes of glitter groupies who can't quite believe that Ali (MacGraw) or Caroline (Kennedy) or Nureyev is less than five feet away.

Fashion begins and ends in this wonderful world of Oz. Its permissive atmosphere encourages extremes in dress. Fashion cognoscenti, back from the latest trip abroad, appear in the most original and amusing styles. And designers are bombarded with new ideas for their next collection. As the disc jockey interweaves hundreds of records, the music grows more insistent, building to climax after climax as glitter dust or multicolored confetti drops from the ceiling. Energized by strobe lights, fantastic backdrops, and pulsating music, the dancers reenact some ancient, infectious tribal rite. They spin like unwound tops; some of them remove their soaked shirts and gyrate until sheer exhaustion and a whiff of amyl nitrite

Two birds of paradise at a fashion fête.

makes them stagger. Truman Capote, one of Studio's habitués, once summed up its attractions for *The New York Times:* "This is the nightclub of the future. It's very democratic. Boys with boys, girls with girls, girls with boys, blacks and whites, capitalists and Marxists, Chinese and everything else—all one big mix!"

The deafening disco beat eradicates the possibility of polite conversation. Those who prefer a bit more intimacy or subscribe to the theory that "contacts are contracts" retreat to the lounge or the womblike balcony over the dance floor. At one party Calvin Klein's introduction to a garment manufacturer ultimately resulted in two million pairs of form-fitting Calvin Klein jeans.

Although many publicists rent Studio 54 to promote a product, owners Ian Schrager and Steve Rubell maintain its air of exclusivity by carefully screening all applicants. Aside from the drama of the space, publicists capitalize on a built-in extra: paparazzi, who make their living shooting stars and selling the pictures, will wait hours to catch a single off-guard expression. To guarantee maximum coverage for a partying designer, his publicist may arrange for him to escort another celebrity with whom he would otherwise never socialize.

When Halston, who loves Studio, arrives with his black-clad pack—illustrator Joe Eula, window designer Victor Hugo, Bianca Jagger, Elsa Peretti, and visiting stars like Diana Ross and Liza Minnelli—the photographers have a field day, and everyone gets coverage.

Carmen D'Alessio, Studio's director of promotion, is famous for her ability to attract a glamorous crowd; she calls her list of eight thousand young, wealthy, and powerful partygoers "the backbone of any club." The Peruvian-born, ebullient D'Alessio gets as much attention as those fortunate enough to be in her files. The fact that she's photographed wherever she goes prompts many designers to offer her their latest creations free or at cost. Although D'Alessio admits that a fashion-show-cum-cocktail-party can cost thousands of dollars (depending on the number of people, the number of drinks, the kind of food, etc.), "Occasionally there are exceptions. When Rubell's close friend Halston or a personality who guarantees the club tremendous publicity throws a party, the rate is adjusted, because publicity is *priceless.*"

Parties to celebrate a designer's or his client's birthday might seem purely festive. They are not. Media coverage of such an event reinforces the designer's status in the public mind and promotes the sale of his more affordable products, usually those available through licensees. Halston's birthday party for Liz Taylor Warner, who wore a purple-sequined Halston design for the occasion, was typically blitzed by the media. Staged for maximum visual effect, the bash featured flowers in vases sculpted from ice, Rockettes prancing onto the dance floor bearing a giant chocolate cake frosted with Liz's likeness and sitting on a bed of forty-six gardenias, and models dancing in Halston dresses. The silver vinyl banquettes were temporarily covered with satin. All the right people were there, including an exotic group of indeterminate gender. When the crowd became overwhelming, Liz took refuge in the disc jockey's booth, Studio's only private spot, where she was permitted to create elaborate effects with the lights.

Valentino also chose Studio 54 for his own fantastic birthday celebration, which featured a circus theme. Some of the guests wore clown costumes from an early Fellini film; others had fanciful makeup applied upon arrival. Clowns and horses cavorted on the sawdust-covered floor, and a golden-haired mermaid on a swing descended from the ceiling to tantalize the partygoers.

Not only does Studio 54 rent out its space to others; from time to time the disco uses it to celebrate itself. Its first anniversary party, "East meets West," attracted four thousand special friends who paid $20 to attend. The event was highlighted by Oriental decor and a dramatic fashion show during which Japanese ceremonial music provided a hypnotic background for Issey Miyake's extraordinary clothes. Later that evening the magnetic Liza Minnelli sang to an admiring crowd.

Another four-star bash was the 1978 Academy Awards party hosted by crowd-drawer Andy Warhol and the newly slim Truman Capote in a straw boater. Studio 54 outdid itself, what with mammoth television screens and still another excuse for some two thousand high-spirited fashionables to put on their most glamorous clothes, whisper intimacies to each other, and see everybody worth seeing. In the middle of the party Mick Jagger and supermodel Jerry Hall raced through the lobby and out the door. Hounded by the zealous paparazzi, they were paying the price of being celebrities. "But it seemed like such a good party," she lamented as the couple of the moment headed toward their limousine parked outside. Other media favorites—model Appolonia in a strapless jumpsuit and twirling a gigantic gold paper fan, Ryan O'Neal in a tropical Hawaiian shirt, and model Barbara Allen in sea-green evening pajamas—danced until dawn before making bird of paradise exits that nearly paralleled their aloof entrances.

But publicity bashes are only one of the tools that a publicist uses to create news about a client; the right article in the right publication is another. Although it is the media's job to tell merchandisers and consumers what's new, it is the publicist working for a designer who informs industry and consumer fashion magazines that a revolutionary new collection deserves instant coverage.*

The press in turn indicates to readers what looks should be avoided (the best method is omission) and what should be purchased. Acting as a liaison between designers, media, and the market, the thorough publicist also works with a designer's advertising agency to ensure that ads appear in publications that provide editorial endorsement. But unlike advertising, publicity has the advantage of appearing as news—or the unvarnished truth.

Although few fashion insiders will go on record about how much politicking occurs before an editor decides which designer merits a garment on a magazine cover, color editorials, or in-depth interviews, a publicist is usually involved. Her professional success rests on a carefully constructed network of media contacts that enables her to bring her client to the public's attention in the best possible light. Occasionally the relationship between an editor and a publicist becomes too close; although reliable sources suggested otherwise, a top fashion paper loudly denied that a highly regarded editor had been fired because of her all-too-chummy relationship with a well-known publicist.

Some designers prefer a full-time in-house publicist to a free-lancer who parcels out her talent to a number of clients. But whether they work for one or several clients, publicists are responsible for setting up interviews; in return for access to a popular designer, a journalist may mention a publicist's up-and-coming client. Capitalizing on a designer's strongest features, a publicist employs a wide range of promotional devices to create the best possible public persona. She balances the number of appearances that a designer makes and the interviews he gives to avoid saturating the media (St. Laurent's infrequent interviews, for example, effectively maintain his aura of inaccessibility.) She tells the press when her client is "dressing" a celebrity. Albert Capraro's White House invitation to create Betty Ford's wardrobe boosted sales from an estimated $2 million to $6 million dollars during his first year in business. McFadden designs

*She eagerly serves up a new line to editors waiting to fill their pages with up-to-the-moment material. If a designer produces a set of futuristic luggage or a new wallpaper matching the prints used for his famous dresses, the publicist sends out photographs and breathless press releases that explain who, what, where, why, and when. Often local editors will be invited to a lavish luncheon or cocktail party to introduce the product in optimal circumstances. If a designer is hot enough, the publicist may have out-of-town press flown in for firsthand coverage.

clothes for Lee Radziwill. Valentino designs for Jackie Onassis; Oscar de la Renta for Pat Buckley; Scaasi for Barbra Streisand. Moreover a publicist will inform the press of her client's upcoming appearances at restaurants, discos, theaters, films, and ballet premieres; when Halston escorted Liz Taylor, wearing a striking, azure-blue chiffon design, to an opening at the Museum of Modern Art and took Jackie Bisset to the disco New York, New York, photographers had a field day.

Just as celebrity endorsements give a product a great boost, the exposure is equally good for a designer appearing in an ad. For this reason Pauline Trigère praises a hideaway bed; Charlotte Ford in one of her own outfits touts a hair treatment; Donna Karan talks about the wonders of rayon. Distinctive-looking designers—including glamorous Diane Von Furstenberg, golden-boy Perry Ellis, rugged Ralph Lauren, porcelain-skinned Gloria Vanderbilt, sexy young Julio, confident Bill Kaiserman,

and aristocratic-looking Halston—are encouraged to appear in advertisements for their products.

A publicist can go so far as to create a complete persona for a designer and instruct him in what to say—and what not to. A clever publicist's responses to queries (how her clients cope with success or with shyness in a room filled with strangers, what they read, where they dine, what they dream) conjure an instant personality for the most inarticulate individuals. Designers are encouraged to join a suitable charity committee and to write books. After Prince Egon Von Furstenberg cowrote *The Power Look,* which guided men on what to wear on what occasion, the public grew more receptive to his latest men's clothing line.

Although each client demands a different approach, the publicity-making process is the same. A case in point is the build-up of Charlotte Ford, the tawny-haired daughter of auto scion Henry Ford II, who joined the growing ranks of socialites-turned-business tycoons. Clothes bearing the label of a woman with enough taste to know what is smart without being ostentatious have immense appeal; as the trenchant Anthony Haden-Guest wrote in *New York* magazine, "Ford is less than a designer, but more than a model; the ultimate choosy consumer."

In 1976, in keeping with her family's time-honored tradition of making money, she assumed the position of fashion director of Charlotte Ford, a division of Don Sophisticates (the powers of Seventh Avenue are not loath to add prestigious names to their companies). She was soon ensconced in a beautiful gray-flannel office, accessorized with hibiscus trees and orchids, in 530 Seventh Avenue (the only other building with cachet is 550 Seventh Avenue).

Although she had never studied design and her only employment had been with a decorating firm for two years, Ford compensated for her lack of practical experience: she hired an in-house design team—a common phenomenon that other designers prefer not to acknowledge—to create casual, classy ensembles that make dressing stylishly easier. Next she recruited Jody Donahue, a top free-lance publicist.

Donahue knew that Ford's upper-class background was a major selling point, especially with customers swayed by names that figure prominently in daily fashion columns. Initially she scheduled a number of store appearances for her new client; later it was decided that the impact of Ford's presence would be reserved for those events that involve an entire community—for example, a benefit for the Lansing, Michigan, Symphony Orchestra. Donahue is also consulted to ensure that Ford's ads, for which the heiress models, exude "a high taste level," and she approves Ford's

Lauren Hutton arriving at the opening of Avedon's one-man
show at the Metropolitan Museum of Art.

endorsements, rejecting products "that don't live up to what she represents."

Gloria Vanderbilt, who inherited $5 million when she was twenty-one, is another of Donahue's clients. When Vanderbilt decided to add fashion to her other commerical design categories, which range from sheets to greeting cards to eyewear, Donahue chose a spectacular setting to launch the medium-priced blouse line. At the Rainbow Room above Rockefeller Center the panoramic view of the city provided a dramatic backdrop for a carefully choreographed show featuring models who carried pony-headed canes and moved along the runway four abreast. Nevertheless Donahue views a fashion show as only a prelude "to a strong merchandising program that includes in-store sales training, proper packaging, and a strong presentation of sufficient stock."

Gloria Vanderbilt's distinct personal style and perennial good looks are an asset when she makes public appearances—so much so that she models her fashions in print and television commercials. "But without a viable commodity and effective follow-through," says Donahue, "even a well-known personality can't make it; the timing and the concept for medium-priced sportswear were right for Gloria Vanderbilt." Though there is little doubt that the right name gives an initial boost to any designer, still, adds Donahue, "Selling is the bottom line."

No single person has done more to sell her clients—some of Seventh Avenue's most renowned—and fashion itself than veteran publicist Eleanor Lambert. Lambert, who regards fashion as "an art form—just as much of an art as theater" and considers herself "someone who swells the audience," is credited with conceptions that draw attention to individual designers as well as to the industry at large: the Coty Awards, the best-dressed list, and press week. In 1942, when World War II made it impossible to buy couture clothes from Paris, the Coty Awards were instituted to recognize American designers for the first time and place them on the fashion map. (In 1979, Coty drew a good deal of criticism from editors and designers for introducing a line of cosmetics entitled "the Coty Awards collection." Calvin Klein and Halston turned down a special citation for focusing the attention of the world on New York fashion designers, awarded only to Hall of Fame members.)

Coty's eleven-year-old Winnie, equivalent to the movie industry's Oscar, is presented each year to American designers of women's and men's clothes; special awards are also given to accessory, lingerie, and fur designers whose work during the previous year has had a significant effect on American fashion. Contestants are nominated by some sixty influential

Halston with Pat Cleveland, one of his favorite models, after a fashion show- cum-dinner party at Bergdorf Goodman's.

members of the New York fashion press such as *Vogue*'s June Weir, head of the nominating committee; *Mademoiselle*'s Edith Locke; *The New York Times*'s Bernadine Morris; the *New York Post*'s columnist Eugenia Sheppard. Some four hundred fifty editors around the country participate in the voting, although some designers complain that many of the out-of-town editors don't see the collections they're judging.

Members of the fashion industry pay $150 each to attend the event, whose proceeds go to the Fashion Institute of Technology's Educational Foundation. As the glittering guests make their entrances, negotiating past throngs of applauding FIT students who ask their favorite designers for autographs, the nominees try to maintain an air of unconcern. The best of each designer's work is usually shown in a brief fashion show. After the winners are announced in an envelope-opening ceremony, guests attend designer-hosted parties ranging from elaborate celebrations in discos to quiet receptions at Seventh Avenue showrooms.

The best-dressed lists honor the world's twelve most stylish women and twelve most stylish men and, by implication, the designers whose clothes they wear. During a meeting chaired by Mrs. Lambert, nominees are selected by ten fashion editors and reporters whose names are kept secret; two thousand ballots are mailed to fashion professionals and socialites all around the world. After ballots are returned, the fashion committee meets in a plush New York hotel. Each name that receives at least one vote is put on an alphabetical list and discussed. In 1978, Bob Colachello, *Interview*'s editor, served on the committee and later repeated some of the more amusing remarks made about the nominees in his column, "Out"; diplomatically he refrained from identifying the speakers. For example, Pat Cleveland was described as "One of the few flat-chested girls who still looks right," Princess Caroline met with, "She dresses awfully." "But we had her on last year." "Even we make mistakes." That year the winners included Ellin Saltzman, Norma Kamali, Paloma Picasso, Diana Ross, Marina Schiano, Jean Muir, Pat Cleveland, and Candice Bergen. Male favorites were Vitas Gerulaitis, John Travolta, President Sadat, Governor Carey, Giorgio Armani, and Prince Egon Von Furstenberg.

Eleanor Lambert's clients are involved, at one time or another, in all these activities; at the same time the doyenne of fashion publicity is in the unique position of writing a fashion-oriented syndicated column. Moreover her office sponsors the twice-yearly "press week" during which out-of-town fashion reporters come to New York to see the latest work of major American designers—many of whom she represents. Mrs. Lambert acknowledges that, "Publicity can build a designer's reputation, although

China Machado—ex-model, ex-senior fashion editor at *Harper's Bazaar*.

it's a designer's fatal error to assume that a magic wand will be waved—and he or she will become an overnight sensation. The real test of success is when a designer's name is mentioned in towns like Shawnee, Oklahoma, and Lafayette, Indiana, as well as in Chicago and San Francisco; then he knows he's really made it.''

As the fashion world's most powerful publicist, Mrs. Lambert is like a Hollywood mogul who works only on high-budget projects. But others in the field will gamble on talented newcomers—and often win. Roz Rubenstein, a new-guard publicist, is one of the whiz kids who breaks all the rules, takes risks, and gets amazing results (especially amazing considering how many of her campaigns are conducted on a shoestring.) Rubenstein developed her skill in spotting and developing talent through years of fashion-related work. In the 1960s she and Stephen Burrows partnered a fabulous boutique; later, she was an accessories buyer for Henri Bendel, managed Halston's Madison Avenue boutique, and joined Stephen Burrows once again as a partner in his Seventh Avenue business. These well-traveled avenues enabled her to meet and befriend many of the press people whom she now deals with on a daily basis. When a magazine needed a fabulous black dress to set off a diamond necklace, the fashion editor knew that a phone call to Rubenstein would result in a half-dozen dresses—in return for designer credit.

Last year Rubenstein promoted Fruit of the Loom fashion T-shirts. The press kit sent to fashion editors included reprints of photographs from European magazines of the "in" bunch wearing the famous fruit logo emblazoned on subtly colored oversized T-shirts. It also contained a color poster of a sensual model in the T-shirt—nothing more, nothing less. Editors were enraptured by this latest fashion find, and trendies bought the shirts by the dozen.

Larger stores maintain their own publicity staff. Instead of concentrating on a specific designer or the promotion of a specific fabric, a department store publicist plans newsworthy events that will build her store's image. Designer appearances are always popular. When Calvin Klein appeared at Saks Fifth Avenue with a dozen male models in his new jeans skipping rope, bouncing on a trampoline, and doing sit-ups, the store, the designer, and the clothes all received favorable publicity. A merchandise happening may be based on a foreign country (Bloomingdale's did a store-wide promotion of Israeli clothes and artifacts last year) or tied in with a current craze (Macy's display staff built a miniature indoor roller-skating rink in a new shop featuring disco-skating clothes and accessories). In-store bashes are popular (Lord and Taylor gave Julio a Creative

A typical couple attending a publicity bash.

Designer Award at a rooftop celebration); so are introductions to a new boutique (members of the fashion industry and the always-on-the-scene fashion groupies toasted Kenzo when he opened a branch of his famous Paris-based "Jap" boutique at Bloomingdale's). Stores may present an educational event ("dress for success" or "more dash than cash" workshops) or set up a restaurant (when Alexander's opened Cafe A'Lex, they held a charity bash featuring a modeling ensemble from Xtazy—a short-lived agency that didn't manage to live up to its name—and enough dessert and cordials to sink the Titanic). Any such endeavor is considered a success if the press covers it or potential customers are attracted to the store.

When Suzi Butterfield, Bergdorf Goodman's stylish and effective publicity director, engineers one of those marvelous fashion shows, the most elegant people in New York turn up—especially after the store began stocking Milanese high-fashion clothes. Last year's more-original-than-ever Fendi fashion show had an audience that nearly rivaled the furs: Anna Bulgari, wife of the famous jeweler; Sant'Angelo, with his infectious high spirits and perpetual tan; Princess Luciana Pignatelli-Avedon, who looks more beautiful each season; Diana Ross, who hummed along with the DJ's selection; and Estée Lauder, who made a grand entrance in jewels and veiled hat seconds before the show began. Bergdorf's received press coverage, and new customers were doubtlessly attracted by the show's Art Deco collage jackets, knitted mink capes, and purple foxes.

Suzi Butterfield once planned an extravagant St. Valentine's Day party for Krizia, whose clothes are sold in one of Bergdorf's boutiques. The atrium of Olympic Towers with its incredible waterfall was the site of a fast-paced benefit fashion show. The models marched out on a specially built platform in the platoon system used so effectively by Milanese designers. Afterward a few hundred fashionables were invited to wear something red to a lavish buffet supper in a rented suite that had been magically transformed into a red Victorian candy box by Larry Laslo, Bergdorf's imaginative display director. Guests included Geoffrey Beene, Chessy Rayner, Valerian Rybar, Scott Barrie, and Bernie Ozer in a heart-patterned Betsey Johnson sweater. The fourth estate was represented by Polly Mellen, Bob Colachello, Jim Brady, and Carrie Donovan. The extensive press coverage pleased Ms. Butterfield, Bergdorf Goodman, and Krizia and compensated for the store's 1978 benefit for the New York City Ballet, which was attended by young fashionables eager to see Armani's latest line; unfortunately a newspaper strike prevented general coverage.

Just as designers and department stores benefit from publicity, a model's name can be a household word. One might suppose that Margaux became an overnight sensation because she is Ernest Hemingway's granddaughter and beautiful as well, but skilled supporters propelled her along at rapid-fire pace.

In 1974, at eighteen, Margaux left Ketchum, Idaho, a cowboy town with one stoplight, for New York to promote a women's free-style championship skiing event on CBS television. Soon after her arrival she met fast-foods entrepreneur Errol Wetson at the Plaza Hotel. Taking her father's advice—"When somebody offers Dom Perignon, say yes"—she accepted Wetson's invitation for champagne. The drink was followed by a weekend together, falling in love, and Margaux's immediate access to that rarefied world populated by top editors and socialites. Halston soon designed clothes for her, and Scavullo photographed her.

Errol Wetson, suave and knowledgeable about who holds power, packaged Margaux as skillfully as his hamburgers. As the couple attended all the best parties, *WWD,* ever on the lookout for a new face with the right name, recorded her every movement. She signed with Wilhelmina and in five months became the most popular face in America. A glowing complexion, radiant smile, and a warm, unselfconscious attitude—and a skilled personal manager-husband—won Margaux her famed Fabergé contract. Luck entered the picture when Fabergé learned that *Time* magazine was planning a story on young beauties; the company pulled together a press conference in record time to announce Margaux's unprecedented million-dollar contract to be paid over three years. The result: a *Time* cover along with television and newspaper coverage that more than repaid the million-dollar outlay. Margaux began making personal appearances in Europe, America, and South Africa. Valerie Jennings, Fabergé's former in-house publicist, spent a great deal of time distributing photos to the press, arranging countless talk show appearances, and ordering "Babe" T-shirts.

An ecstatic Margaux and Errol celebrated their good fortune by getting married. Soon the jet-set wunderkind starred in her first film, *Lipstick,* which did not exactly receive rave reviews. In 1978, four years after their magical meeting, the idyllic marriage ended in divorce. Margaux fell in love with a sophisticated Venezuelan film maker; an accelerated involvement in movie making seems to have diminished her interest in fashion modeling. If she decides to make a comeback, however, any number of publicists will happily promote her career.

Although it is impossible to measure the effect that publicity has on sales, there is little doubt that wise use of the media shapes public opinion and develops a person's or product's image. The reader will have to decide which is more important—the show or the ringmaster.

FASHION MOVERS

THE WOMEN WHO WEAR THE CLOTHES

"Style has to do with the way
you go to bed at night, with the way
you eat, what you eat. Everything you do in life has style."

—Marisa Berenson, *Vogue*

As she enters the trendy restaurant, wearing a black smoking suit and trailing a magnificent fox coat, no one fails to notice her. She knows this. She is one of the fashion movers, well aware that photographs of her will be seen by thousands here and across the world. What she wears affects legions of fashion followers as well as the designers who look to her for inspiration.

A fashion mover thrives on style. With an infallible sensitivity to upcoming trends she knows what's new before anyone else has a clue. She loves to discover out-of-the-way places and promote designers by displaying their clothes at public events. She knows exactly how to optimize her looks; if she isn't beautiful, she is at least dramatic, and you'll see her dressed in a slashed-to-the-waist tuxedo worn without a shirt; a black-and-white striped dress accented by black gloves; an oversized man's T-shirt with skintight leather jeans; or a diaphanous black chiffon dress set off by a sequin-pavéed bolero jacket. Whether her look is elegant, whimsical, or just expensive, she is never less than porcelain-perfect. She might discard lovers or friends, but she would never abandon style. As Diana Vreeland told *Vogue,* "I don't think you can have it one day and not the next. You have it getting into bed. You have it when you have a temperature of 103° and are moaning. It's you—that's all your style is. Whatever you have comes out of your style."

The style setters are concerned with more than clothes, however; where to go and with whom are equally crucial decisions, and the right connections—with the ultimate rock star or hottest photographer, stage designer, choreographer, ballet dancer, playwright, painter—are imperative. Traveling with an entourage of narcissistic, pansexual young men with high cheekbones who are as visually oriented (if not more so) than

Margaux Hemingway—Fabergé's supermodel.

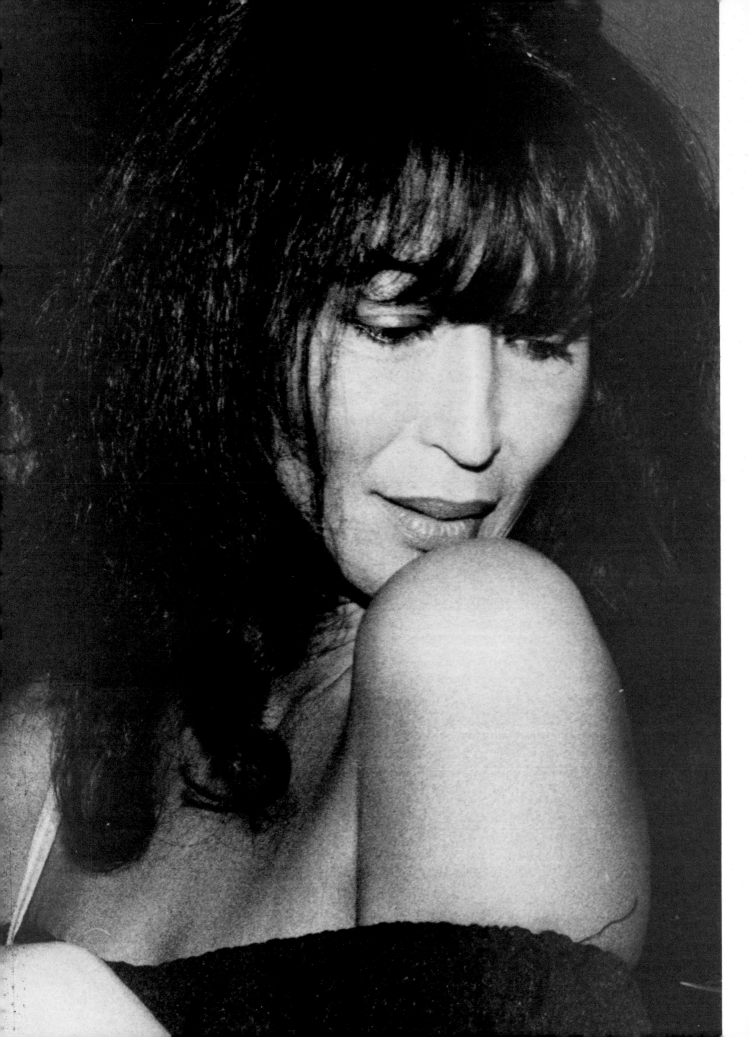

Caterine Milinaire (author of *Birth*, coauthor of *Cheap Chic,* and former youth editor of *Vogue*): "Fashion is fun and a luxury: life would be totally dull if you didn't explore the possibility of expressing yourself through clothes."

---

themselves, those vain aristocrats of the night move without pause from one party to another. As the less attractive watch, attempting hopelessly to comprehend the never-to-be understood essence of their style, the fashion pack makes yet another collective razzle-dazzle entrance at yet another event.

What the fashionables ate, with whom they danced, what they wore, what witticisms they uttered (at a recent posh dinner a jet-setting designer discussed the relative merits of solid versus patterned men's socks)—all are recorded for a vast and spellbound audience. When they appear at a disco or a restaurant on several consecutive evenings, the establishment's owner or publicist informs the press that the right people are in the right place (his place) at the right time (now). Fashion groupies follow the media to the newest, trendiest hangout, hoping to catch a glimpse of their favorite style setters. Inevitably, by the time they arrive, the restless fashion movers have decamped to a more amusing, even newer spot.

Although every major city can boast a contingent of these iridescent, attention-craving creatures, those in New York flash from one event to another at a pace unmatched elsewhere. Fashionables have a knack of remaining unruffled no matter what happens around them. And no matter where they travel, they're armed with the addresses of others of their ilk. Fashion is and always has been the code language of status; just as Englishmen of a certain class recognize one another by their ties—public school, regiment, or club—fashionables communicate through a sweater casually draped across the shoulders, a window-pane-checked scarf wrapped around a waist, a sable-lined trench coat, a 1940s striped chenille jacket.

A sense of style extends into every area of the fashion movers' lives. Fashion prompts their appearance at a little-known but very "in" vacation spot, the hottest transvestite bar, high-tech decor, or the right restaurant. As irrational as it may seem, food is not a critical factor in the popularity of the restaurant of the moment. Fashionables pick a place that serves as a perfect backdrop for themselves and their clothes. As Mimi Sheraton, food critic for *The New York Times,* observed, "What most people look for is the 'total experience,' a chance to play a role in the living theater that a

China Machado.

Daniela Morera: "European women don't make dressing a career; Kempner's career seems to be to dress in couture clothes. Perhaps she is more profound. I think, though, that she's another example of America's creation of a heroine overnight, an enormous personality because she dresses well."

restaurant truly is. With the fashion world turning to costumes that permit one to be a peasant today and a study in 1940s nostalgia tomorrow, one needs a variety of settings in which to play out the role of the moment."

The right crowd may frequent a particular restaurant because it is owned by a friend or touted by an ambitious publicist who threw an extravagant opening-night party to attract an all-important nucleus of fashionables. They favor a unique, sophisticated atmosphere (One Fifth Avenue features the salvaged Art Deco interior of a first-class ocean liner) or a gracious one (La Grenouille is appreciated for magnificent fresh flowers and impeccable service). And they enjoy chic establishments like Le Relais, 21, or Orsini's that are populated by other glamorous people.

Private restaurants are also popular. For example, Doubles, located in the depths of the luxurious Sherry-Netherland Hotel, is frequented by international society. Members like Nan Kempner, Maggie Newhouse, C. Z. Guest, and Pat Buckley can relax in the knowledge that anyone else there is of their privileged sort.

For the past several years Elaine's has been one of the ultimate "in" restaurants in Manhattan. On any given night its unobtrusive decor is enlivened by a glittery crowd of film makers, actors, and writers; pasta invariably tastes better when it's enjoyed a table or two away from Warren Beatty, Diane Keaton, George Plimpton, or Cheryl Tiegs. Mortimer's is another hangout long favored by the fashionables; Diana Vreeland, Helmut Berger, William Paley, and Charlotte Ford are some of its habitués. Mortimer's sophisticated, chain-smoking owner, Glen Bernbaum, is not a typical restaurateur; he attended prep school, is a Princeton graduate, and has three or four "socially prominent friends as my customers."

Although fashion movers can afford to eat at the most luxurious restaurants, they descend on the unpretentious Mortimer's for their ritual Saturday and Sunday brunch. "There are a few who tend to overestimate their importance," Bernbaum admits, "but most fashionables are far less demanding than others. They feel like it's their restaurant; if they don't get their ashtrays emptied, they aren't upset." He describes Mortimer's fare as "simple, nicely prepared food for the rich. It's the same food that their cooks served them when they were children—or that they ate at the country club."

Woods, another restaurant frequented by the fickle fashion pack, is owned by the kinetic Zeus Goldberg, whose fashion-business background made the transition in occupations easier. "I feed who I clothed," he points out. "I know what they want as soon as they do." Because he considers Woods "a Madison Avenue food boutique," Goldberg regularly changes the menu and redecorates the windows. And because "the food is the color palette," he uses only simple china. Among the patrons who appreciate his untiring attention to detail are Calvin Klein, Perry Ellis, and Marina Schiano. But despite Goldberg's concern about the well-being of his clientele, his patience *was* tried when an Argentinian woman demanded a glass of strained water. Perhaps she considered it fashionable.

An almost religious dedication to fashion is not unique to contemporary society. What is unique—and astounding—is the celebrityhood conferred on these superconsumers by the media that knows that fashion chitchat sells magazines and newspapers; no student of style would miss *WWD*'s "Eye" column. The fashion movers do not exactly object to the attention. It would become monotonous if they had only each other for whom to preen. (As one perennial jetsetter remarked, "I keep seeing the same people I see in Paris, St. Moritz, Monte Carlo, and Rio. I don't know if I'm following them or they're following me.") The slavish devotion of photographers who follow in their wake affords fashionables the luxurious sensation of basking in the limelight with perpetual smiles tattooed on their famous faces. Those smiling faces often serve as impenetrable facades. As Andy Warhol noted, "During the sixties people forgot what emotions were supposed to be, and I don't think they've ever remembered."

With or without fixed smiles fashion movers fall into two distinct categories. The first comprises amusing young self-starters with an instinctive sense of style who absorb everything they see on their constant travels. With supreme self-assurance they scour antique shops for one-of-a-kind accessories (lace-encrusted satin camisoles, cashmere shawls, hand-tooled leather belts with silver buckles); mix clothes from different periods, and

Kenzo told *W*: "What bores me is the life of fashion people who take themselves seriously."

Marc Bohan told *Interview*: "Marisa Berenson has a strong personality; clothes don't overwhelm her. Marisa doesn't look the same every single evening . . . I like this very much."

add custom-made boots to create an individualistic look that's always up-to-date. Style setters of this sort may be well-known from birth or through their talent, their beauty, their marriages, or a combination thereof. In this group one finds model-actresses Marisa Berenson, Margaux Hemingway, and Bianca Jagger; socialites Yasmin Khan, Delfina Ratazzi, Diane de Beauvau, and Andrea de Portago; and models-turned-career-women like Marina Schiano, who heads YSL's operations in America, film stylist China Machado, and fashion correspondent and art director Daniela Morera. This list also includes socialite-turned-designer Diane Von Furstenberg (who rarely socializes in her trademark wrap-around dress), free-lance publicist Carmen D'Alessio, who is as exuberant as a fireworks' display, and the divine Paloma Picasso. No matter what they wear, these women and others like them embody style—and use it to great advantage.

Bianca Jagger has made a career out of being photographed, alone or with a coterie of admirers (Mick always seemed to be just a continent away), in what amounts to a long-running documentary study of her unique fashion sense. Aided and abetted by her share of her ex-husband's $20 million fortune, she appeared in flawlessly tailored English suits with matching bowlers and canes—a look that catapulted her into the ranks of international trendsetters. More recently she's favored plump fox scarves color-keyed to sleek gowns by Halston (her favorite American designer and her host during her New York visits) and the flouncing femininity of Marc Bohan's crinoline-shaped ball gowns undoubtedly inspired by *Gone With the Wind*. In between rearing her young daughter Jade and flitting around the world, Bianca has lent her seductive beauty to two films not yet commercially distributed. Whether the Nicaraguan-born former wife of a demigod is as strong an actress as her visual presence promises remains to be seen.

Marisa Berenson, an aloof, high-strung beauty, is another paparazzi favorite. Having learned the essentials of high style from Madame Schiaparelli, her famous couturier grandmother, and never having forgotten them, Marisa has always behaved like a star. As a young and highly successful model she posed for top fashion photographers and traveled around the world on assignments. At twenty-six, when modeling began to bore her, she made her film debut in *Cabaret*. Her next and last movie,

Fashion mover par excellence—Jackie Onassis.

Victor Hugo (artist): "Bianca is one of the most intelligent and romantic women I've ever met."

Barry Lyndon, showed her to advantage aesthetically; her performance, however, left something to be desired emotionally.

In between acting stints Marisa remained in the news through a highly publicized romance with a member of the illustrious Rothschild family. After her short-lived marriage (even by Hollywood standards) to Jim Randall, the millionaire owner of a Beverly Hills palazzo, she was injured in a 1978 car crash that necessitated plastic surgery. Her face restored to pristine splendor, Marisa appeared at a party in her honor at Xenon. To celebrate her visit to New York, the disco was decorated with huge photo stills capturing her famous style in everything from extravagant furs to fanciful picture hats. But beneath her thousand-watt smile is a trace of vulnerability, a world-weariness that she, like so many other fashionables, conceals with brocade suits, marabou jackets, and resplendent jewels.

Although top model and actress Lauren Hutton based her career on making elegant clothes appear even more elegant, fashion is not her major concern. Away from the camera Lauren prefers anonymity. On strolls through her Greenwich Village neighborhood, dressed in crew-neck sweaters and washed-out jeans, she nevertheless is seen—and scrutinized. After she wore bright Hawaiian print shirts, every fashion freak had to have a similar one, and she made sneakers respectable long before jogging became a fad.

When Princess Diane de Beauvau arrived in New York from Paris, her title and business connection with Halston guaranteed her instant access to all the amusing people. Daring Diane predated those would-be punk rockers. Wearing her hair short and slicked back, she appeared in black satiny bodysuits, dark glasses à la Halston, black Springolator heels, and long slinky gloves.

When the infinitely stylish Diane Von Furstenberg hit New York in 1970 with her husband, Prince Egon Von Furstenberg, she immediately joined a free-wheeling party scene frequented by good-looking, languid Europeans and South Americans famed for immaculately cut suits and enigmatic business connections. It was not long before she and Egon were voted "The couple of the year" by *New York* magazine (Amanda and Carter Burden shared the title and, make of it what you will, both couples separated soon afterward).

Moments before a fashion show featuring Krizia's designs.

One of Bergdorf Goodman's larger-than-life mannequins.

(*l. to r.*) Millie Kaiserman, Bernardo Foucher, and Margaux Hemingway.

Pat Cleveland (*l.*) and Jan Stevenson stepping out in Krizia fashions at the Olympic Towers.

Artist Victor Hugo and one of his favorite ladies, Bianca Jagger.

Beauteous Marina Schiano, director of YSL operations in America, at the Metropolitan Museum of Art's Costume Institute.

Wearing YSL, fashionable Nan Kempner poses in her Park Avenue duplex.

Diana Vreeland, doyenne of the fashion world and director of the Metropolitan Museum's Costume Institute, savors another successful show.

Bob Currie, Bendel's jet-hopping visual planner, applies the finishing touches.

Larry Laslo, Bergdorf Goodman's window display director, surveys Fifth Avenue from his special vantage point.

(Opposite page) *Vogue* Editor-in-Chief Grace Mirabella congratulates Halston on his latest showing.

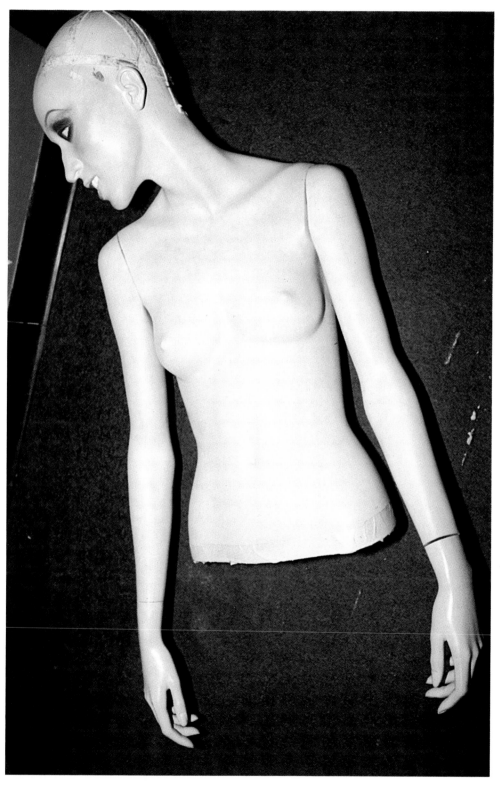

A mannequin of superstar model
Pat Cleveland—now appearing in
windows around the world.

Wilhelmina adjusts the
hair of one of her young
models.

International model Sayoko gets
ready to show one of Dianne B.'s
latest designs.

(Opposite page) One of
Studio 54's habitués.

Andy Warhol relaxes at Studio 54 with Doris Duke.

Exuberant Studio 54 co-owner Steve Rubell (*l.*) with Halston.

(Opposite page) Rita undergoes the last back-stage adjustments before showing the latest style from Dianne B.

Fabulous Billie Blair is made up before Kansai Yamamoto's fashion show.

Exaggerated makeup heightens Sayoko's delicate features.

A striking Beverly Johnson waits for a cue.

Pat Cleveland shows Halston's taffeta suit in
his sumptuous Olympic Towers showroom.

Chris Royer shows Halston.

A Bergdorf Goodman window designed by Larry Laslo.

The democratic Egon urged Diane to fill her time by working. Soon the young Belgian-born socialite enjoyed incredible success, first by designing textile prints and a basic wrap dress that women appreciated for its practicality and sexiness, and then via her $18 million cosmetics and fragrance business and the licensing agreements that bring in $5.5 million annually. The fact that the Von Furstenbergs were the most attractive and titled couple at parties populated by influential editors and publicists like Eugenia Sheppard and Earl Blackwell did not hurt her career.

After her divorce Diane retained her mediagenic appeal. The public was aware that she purchased twenty pairs of Dior point d'esprit tights in Paris, jogged down Fifth Avenue accompanied by a limousine bearing her work clothes, and received twenty-seven uncut diamonds from her close friend Barry Diller, chairman of Paramount pictures. Her décolleté dresses and gorgeous glitter-strewn jackets, topped by a striking face and wild frizzy hair, make Diane Von Furstenberg the kind of fashion celebrity whom millions of women never tire of emulating—even if only by buying a pair of her initialed sunglasses.

Loulou Klossowski, the unofficial "Madame St. Laurent," is the world-renowned designer's assistant and muse. Loulou puts together bits and pieces of fabrics and jewels and creates uncanny effects. Her pre-Raphaelite beauty and innate sense of the dramatic have thrust her to the top of the list of international fashion makers.

Daniela Morera, a high-spirited individualist who divides her time between Milan and New York, is one taste setter who doesn't appear on the pages of fashion magazines. Instead top international designers invite her to organize elaborate fashion events; to complement Bill Kaiserman's contemporary clothes, she found the perfect architectural site, Pier 54, and staged a brilliant show complete with live drummers and fake palm trees. European and Japanese magazines hire her to write articles and design covers. An inveterate world traveler with a well-developed eye for detail, Daniela is often inspired by indigenous fashion; a corset under a shirt in Bali or the pegged pants worn by workmen in Kashmir, for example, may be adapted and added to her wardrobe. A year later her ideas

Phyllis Tweel (journalist): "Bianca Jagger was put in the spotlight because of Mick. I think that it's impossible to survive on someone else's image. Wearing clothes isn't enough. You have to be productive."

Phyllis Tweel: "Marisa Berenson is feminine and glamorous. She has the poise and class to complete what she's about."

will reappear in various designers' collections—with acknowledgments to Daniela.

With her talent for combining designer clothes with flea-market finds, Daniela consistently creates fabulous outfits. And when she finds flattering clothes and accessories, she will order several variations of each. One visit to Maud Frizon's shoe factory in Italy made her an instant fan; long before they were considered fashionable, Daniela wore—and continues to wear—Frizon's high-heeled ankle straps in every imaginable color and texture.

Although Daniela is aware of her impact on designers and admirers who imitate her style, a number of fashion movers are oblivious of the impression they make as they saunter down a street or enter a still undiscovered restaurant. Some of them are fashion models who avoid wearing a particular designer's clothes to spare the sensibilities of the others; instead they look marvelous in an eclectic mixture of the antique and the ethnic acquired on frequent bookings around the world. Other models buy garments wholesale or receive them as gifts from designers who know the impact of a Pat Cleveland or a Margaux Hemingway seen in their clothes; and some might borrow a spectacular dress for a special media-covered event.

But mostly they are anonymous, these delicious-looking trendsetters who arrive at a disco long past midnight in a ruffled rhumba skirt or clinging leopard-stenciled bodysuit, with a clutter of metallic pins decorating a stark gabardine jacket or with a batik scarf worn as a bandeau. As they hurl themselves across the dance floor, they are watched by a handful of aficionados who absorb their message long before the ink dries on the pages of *WWD*. Having earned the appreciation of designers who sometimes adapt their fashion ideas into the new line, these glorious creatures disappear into the night.

Somewhat older, more sedate, and not at all anonymous, fashion movers in the second category belong to that gilded infantry that marches across the pages of *Women's Wear Daily*. Betsey Bloomingdale, D. D. Ryan, Lee Radziwill, Pat Buckley, Chessy Rayner, Mica Ertegun, Jackie Onassis, Françoise de la Renta, Estée Lauder, and Nan Kempner are among the trendsetters photographed at charity balls, intimate publishing parties, and fashion shows wearing beautifully cut, understated clothes from their

Lee Radziwill with Studio 54 co-owner Steve Rubell.

Phyllis Tweel: "Nan Kempner is a fashion mover, because there's no one else around, and Eugenia Sheppard and *WWD* accept what she's doing."

favorite Seventh Avenue designers or French couturiers; the press coverage they command (sometimes prompted by a publicist) inspires wealthy but less tasteful women who, substituting money for individual style, purchase similar designs.

Many of these "golden ladies" subscribe to the work ethic described by Charlotte Curtis, the Op-Ed page editor of *The New York Times,* in *W:* "Work is the chic of the week. Anybody who wants to be considered at all must work—or at least do something for which she appears to get paid." To earn their keep (or to seem to), they design interiors and accessories for a clientele as wealthy as they, labor as consulting editors (fashion or otherwise), or control cosmetics empires.

Some, of course, merely devote their time to themselves. Current or former superwealthy husbands provide the money they require to remain timeless fixtures in the fashion firmament. Midday, the unemployed "inner circle" can be found at La Caravelle, La Grenouille, and other midtown French restaurants where they receive preferential treatment while lunching on infinitely small portions of salmon and watercress sprinkled with the kind of juicy gossip that Truman Capote uses to such advantage in "Answered Prayers." Then they dash home for private exercise and massage appointments, change into even more divine outfits, and meet again, with male escorts, later in the evening. Their fervently affectionate greetings suggest that they haven't seen each other for months rather than hours. If they are not attending a museum or ballet opening, they are hosting intimate dinners in plush apartments where impeccably served food is enjoyed by impeccably attired guests.

Along with the press, three hundred buyers, and private European customers like Catherine Deneuve, Paloma Picasso, Helene Rochas, and Marie Hélène de Rothschild, most fashion ladies attend the Paris haute couture collections at least twice per year. They jot down the numbers of the most appealing outfits, order them, and return for three or more fittings over three weeks until the $2,000 coat or $1,500 embroidered gown they've chosen accentuates their best features and minimizes their worst ones. Alterations are made on mannequin forms of the designers' clientele while the women themselves attend parties given by renowned hostesses like Régine or make quick jaunts to a spa for rejuvenating waters

and healthy mountain air. The resulting garments often bear no relation to the original samples (which might have taken more than one hundred fifty hours of hand sewing to complete).

Jackie Onassis is the classic fashion mover. Neither anorexic nor androgynous, she projects an innocence and engaging individual style that enhances her beauty. Her predilection for deceptively simple, magnificently cut clothes was exemplified by the white pleated Mary McFadden gown she wore to the media-covered preview of the Russian-costumes exhibit at the Metropolitan Museum of Art. Because of their great faith in Jackie's taste, dating back to her tenure at the White House, affluent women who think nothing of spending $1,200 on a single garment immediately ordered similar dresses. She became a formidable fashion influence when she accompanied her first husband on a state visit to Charles de Gaulle. Her signature pillbox hat by Halston and her simple wool coat by Oleg Cassini won over the fastidious French press, which also appreciated her diplomatic gesture in wearing a jeweled gown by Givenchy, one of Paris's great couturiers, to a state dinner. Upon her return to America Jackie was instantly emulated by hordes of women across America who studied her hair, makeup, and understated clothes.

One of the "golden ladies" who illustrates the dictum that slender is synonymous with fashionable is Nan Kempner. A charming, high-keyed woman who maintains a permanent tan, Kempner compulsively attends most fashion and social events; her fear that the one she might be missing is more exciting than the one she's at results in a round of party going that would leave most people totally exhausted. Choosing from a veritable bouquet of invitations, she puts in an appearance at cocktail parties ("Fine when I'm on my way somewhere else."); gallery openings ("If there are very good paintings, I like first choice."); dinners ("Trained diplomats make the best conversationalists."); disco-skating parties or whatever else may be happening.

Kempner, who considers her fast-paced life an antidote to aging, indulges in water- and snow skiing, swimming, sailing, and cosmetic surgery ("It's like cutting my cuticles.") to keep her looking young and attractive. On the rare occasions when she stays home, she pores over menus with her cook to plan detail-perfect luncheons and dinner parties. One month, when over three hundred people were invited to a variety of lunches, she thought about installing a turnstile. To relax, she takes weekend trips to her remodeled barn in upstate New York, where guests are told, "No shoes. No ties." But in Manhattan, dressed in a stunning, deceptively simple suit, and about to embark on another evening's entertainment, she's likely to comment, "The best party was yesterday's—until this evening."

Kempner was elected to the Fashion Hall of Fame after appearing on the best-dressed list for three years. Her unrelenting passion for beautiful clothes dates back to her childhood, when her perfectionist mother and grandmother turned her out in exquisitely matched outfits; even then she was the most elegantly dressed student at her private girls' school in San Francisco. Today she attends the haute couture showings two or three times a year, ordering clothes from her favorite designers—Yves St. Laurent, Bohan, Ungaro, and Madame Grès. As a woman who personifies high chic, she instinctively knows what will work with her extensive wardrobe, and she usually selects "this year's version of last year's clothes."

Phyllis Tweel: "I think that Monique [Van Vooren] is a mover; she's gone through many stages of life, has never once given up doing things. She writes, sings, and is concerned with her vanity."

Bill Kaiserman: "I think that Daniela Morera could be a great producer, politician, or designer. Many designers would like her to devote time to their cause. She's a supercreative person."

The closets of her enormous bedroom in an art-filled Park Avenue duplex have timeless originals that she wears until they are "threadbare"; at that point she relegates them to a special box destined for the Metropolitan Museum of Art's Costume Institute. Although there's no doubt that clothes are Kempner's priority, she does find time to work. As a fashion correspondent for French *Vogue,* she focuses on discos, amusing stores, restaurants, or fat farms. "When the occasion arises," she also works for Harry Platt of Tiffany's, helping to correlate the store's jewelry purchases with the latest European fashion looks; décolleté dresses demand chokers, for example, while a high neckline is best enhanced with chains.

Kempner recalls one evening when she looked especially glamorous at a party and couldn't help thinking, "It's such a pity that *Women's Wear* isn't here." It was also unusual: *WWD*'s photographer is rarely more than a few steps behind her as she makes one of her electrifying entrances swathed in black broadtail edged with luxuriant silver fox or wearing a beaded jacket over a backless reed-slim gown. Her definition of style encompasses most of her interests: "Style is how you put yourself together and carry it off. It is also connected to a life-style embodying a sensitivity to marvelous objects, good food, beautiful music. It takes less time than you might expect. Too many American women are badly dressed because they either believe the publicity attached to a designer who isn't right for them, or they simply don't know what's suitable for them."

Unlike her husband, an investment banker who shuns publicity, Kempner admits, "When approached by anyone with a camera, I smile broadly from ear to ear on all occasions." Although she adds that she would "knock over children and grandmothers to be photographed," she views fashion as the frosting on the cake. "I love getting dressed up and being admired. It's a great ego trip. Actually, I feel desperately vulnerable." She pauses reflectively. "There is always a certain sensitivity that goes with a love of beautiful things. Part of being fashionable comes out of insecurity, and then all the attention makes it snowball. Underneath the bravado, most fashionable women are actually marshmallows."

CHAPTER SIX

THE PHOTOG-RAPHER

STOP-ACTION WIZARD

"Every woman who steps in front
of my camera is the most glamorous
and desirable woman on earth."

—A prominent photographer

antastic! I love it!" Click. "Do that again." Click. "Terrific! Great!"
Click. "Okay. Okay. That's enough." One of America's most successful
photographers (better known than many of his subjects) hands his camera
to one assistant and ten rolls of film to another. He's just shot an upcoming *Cosmopolitan* cover featuring strawberry-blond supermodel Patti Hansen. After a lunch break another dazzling model arrives at the studio for a
beauty editorial. "Fabulous! I'm coming in on you." Click. "Like that—
perfect! Great!" Click. "Okay. Okay. That's enough."

The freewheeling life of the fashion photographer, punctuated by
scenes very much like this, fascinated the audience in Antonioni's unfor-
gettable film, *Blow-Up.* Its attractive, insatiably curious hero sped through
the swinging London of the 1960s, taking pictures and cavorting with
gorgeous nymphets and sophisticated women. The movie inspired hundreds of young photographers yearning for a career whose modest income can skyrocket to $350,000 a year while providing opportunities for
world travel and bed partners of either sex.

Though many novices are attracted by the excitement of the scene, the
wiser ones realize that only years of hard work and discipline bring fame
and fortune. However, in a field where change is the one constant, it is
possible for photographers with technical skill, good taste, and an ability
to establish a rapport with clients and models to produce celebrated work
that takes the pulse of the times. What distinguishes the artists from the
technicians is a transcendent quality, an obsession with visual perfection
that results in distinctive editorial and advertising shots.

The fashion photography found in magazines captures a mood or a
sense of drama and projects the image of the publication: *Town & Country*
emphasizes old money, for example, while *Gentlemen's Quarterly* stresses

The author at Halston's show. Photograph by Yorgos Galazidis.

sophistication, and *Good Housekeeping* displays a down-to-earth fashion sense. The atmosphere desired for a fashion story will dictate an editor's choices among the shots provided; as long as a photographer stays within the magazine's general boundaries, he has license to create pictures with his individual look. If American *Vogue* wants the free-spirited look of long-legged women dashing across the street, Arthur Elgort is a likely candidate; if French *Vogue* prefers an implicitly violent or decadent situation, Helmut Newton is an excellent prospect.

An editorial assignment rarely pays as well as an advertising job. Nevertheless a photographer willingly accepts a fee of $150 to $450, depending on the magazine's prestige and circulation and his own status, for that all-important credit line that enables potential clients with large advertising budgets to identify his work.

On the other hand, photography for fashion advertising involves far more planning and, usually, less freedom. Guided by story-board illustrations, the photographer must follow detailed instructions and obey an art director who ensures that the product is paramount and that the picture appeal to a mass rather than select audience. Because his fee is only a small percentage of the total budget, an advertising agency pays a photographer up to $3,000 to $4,000 to produce a powerful image that will appear in a number of national magazines. Advertising campaigns can run into the millions; Martin, Stertevant, Silverman, and Marshall, the agency that handles Von Furstenberg cosmetics and fragrance, bills $1.2 million on that account alone. The costliness of a campaign and the necessity to emphasize the product make it rare for a client to credit the photographer. One of the exceptions to this rule is Chicago-based Victor Skrebneski, whose credit line does appear on ads. His most famous advertising account is a long-running series for Estée Lauder cosmetics featuring Karen Graham, an icy beauty, in sumptuous settings (often Skrebneski's own treasure-filled apartment).

Catalogs are another form of advertising that photographers regard as lucrative but not very imaginative work. Called "rack 'em in, rack 'em out" in the industry, the shots may require a week of constant shooting;

China Machado (film stylist, runs the Glamour Institute): "Avedon has a special magic, a distinctive style that everyone tries to copy. No one can touch him. He has always chronicled the times, and never photographed statically . . . Guy Bourdin has a special quality. He is a little strange and appeals to a viewer's darker side."

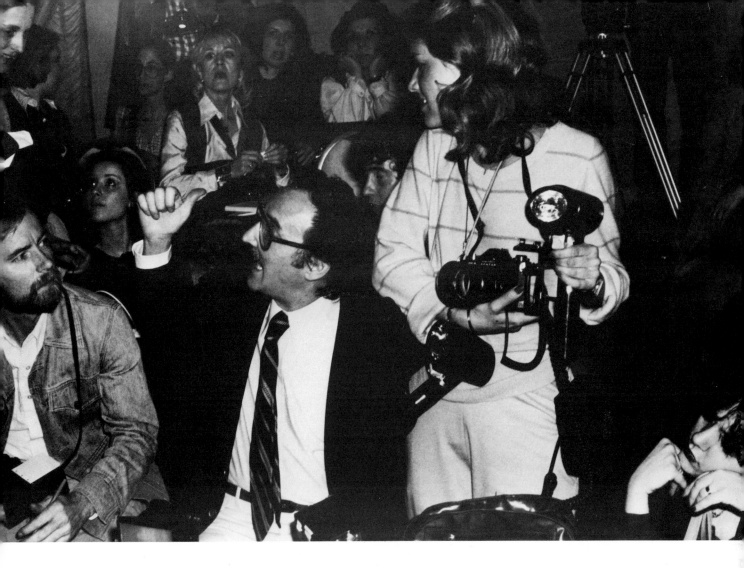

the models make eight or ten changes a day. Because catalogs reach an audience that bought some $22 billion in mail-order merchandise last year, it's inevitable that they have become more sophisticated. In 1977, Bloomingdale's hired Guy Bourdin to shoot a Christmas lingerie mailer. His contract specified that there would be no art director and no reshoots. He used sensuous young models in provocative poses, presented the striking results to Bloomingdale's, and left for Paris. The catalog, sent only to charge customers on the Upper East Side, caused a bit of a furor; while some customers considered it brilliant, others threatened to burn their charge plates. In 1978, Avedon produced another memorable Christmas catalog for Bloomingdale's.

Other department stores soon began to offer more imaginative books of their own. Saks Fifth Avenue's art director, Len Restivo, selects different photographers to give each catalog a special look. Restivo determines the mood that he wants, finds a location to reflect that mood, and lets the photographer do the rest. Although he provides guidance and controls major elements, one of the factors out of his control is the weather; at a

Fran Lebowitz (author of *Metropolitan Life*): "I love fashion photographers, because they're frankly artificial. There's no myth about stepping down to reality."

recent shoot on a Greek island chosen for its beauty and warm climate, unexpected gale-force winds forced the crew to complete the shoot indoors.

No matter how skilled the photographer, the success of a fashion photograph depends on the right model. Although any woman with good features can be transformed into a beauty for photographic purposes through lighting, makeup, hairstyling, and retouching, a perfectionist demands that a model have good skin, large and expressive eyes, a swanlike neck, and a charisma that sets her apart.

Wherever a photographer goes, he keeps an eye out for a magnetic new face. When he spots one, he arranges a shooting to determine if she's photogenic. Peter Beard, jet-set traveler famed for his photos of African game preserves, created quite a stir when he revealed that he had found Iman, a statuesque African beauty, herding cattle in a remote Kenyan bush. It was discovered later that she was actually the daughter of a manager of the Nairobi Hilton. Those with a trained eye can often spot modeling potential; several years ago a photographer discovered fifteen-year-old Patti Hansen at a hot-dog stand on Staten Island. Still most photographers admit that they aren't always aware of how special a woman can look until they see her on film.

Some photographers prefer working with models with whom they've already established a rapport, who respond immediately and assume the right attitude with minimum direction. Others derive a Pygmalion-like satisfaction from discovering a new model, teaching her how to stand and what to do with her hands, eliciting subtle changes in her expression—in short, molding her like clay. Barry Lategan, whose reputation was made when he photographed Twiggy, "the face of 1966," acquired a reputation for his ability to extract more from inexperienced models. As he told Charles Castle in *Model Girl,* "In the beginning, girls don't really know what they should look like, and so they present themselves in a nice open way to the camera. Obviously they are manipulated by me. I find it harder to work with them after a time when they have seen the success of a photo, examined it, and then parody what they see. It's kind of a narcissistic repetition, and then I can no longer extend them. And so, sadly, as fashion goes on, I move to another girl."

A professional model has been taught the art
of making up to accentuate her best features.

Whether a prospective picture is for fashion editorial or advertising purposes, the assignment can be broken down into preshooting, on site, and postshooting stages. Before the shoot the model must be selected. After poring through agency head sheets and models' composites and conferring with an art director, the photographer selects a dozen possibilities. The agencies involved then send the models' portfolios to the art director, who makes the final decision.

While learning his craft, the photographer's assistant, like the designer's assistant, takes care of the less glamorous details. He books the model tentatively for a particular date and time; the confirmed booking is made at least forty-eight hours before the shooting. When three or more models are used, scheduling becomes complicated; a last-minute television commercial or a week in the Bahamas may be offered to one of them, and the substitute suggested by the agency may not complement the others. The assistant also assembles the camera equipment and checks the weather forecast. Exterior work requires a "weather permit," which means booking two dates so the shoot can be rescheduled in case of bad weather (a model is paid half her fee for the canceled date plus full pay for the actual shooting).

Another person key to a shooting is the stylist, who works on a free-lance basis or full time for a photographer. To evoke the mood the photographer wants to convey, she borrows or rents props, clothes, and accessories. An experienced stylist is familiar with Seventh Avenue resources. She knows exactly which manufacturer makes an immaculately tailored cream-colored suit that will be a perfect foil for a "new" shade of raspberry lipstick and nail polish. She will also scour antique and specialty shops for a beige tufted-velvet sofa and make countless calls to plastic manufacturers for a rare see-through raft, the perfect prop for an upcoming bathing suit ad.

Kezia Keeble, half of the only free-lance stylist couple in New York, has spent the last eighteen years behind the scenes aiding photographers. The strangest prop she ever borrowed was a ten-foot python Richard Avedon needed for an exercise shot illustrating the principle of expansion and contraction. Keeble remembers the extraordinary tension of watching the python wrap itself around Lauren Hutton's throat.

David McCabe (photographer): "It's the easiest and best-paid job in the world; you get to travel with beautiful women, and three meals a day are thrown in. What more can I ask for?"

If he can't find an appropriate site for a particular shot, a photographer will use the services of a location stylist. For $75 the stylist scours an extensive file of hard-to-find spots and selects a private house overlooking an extravagant garden or, to approximate the feeling of London, a coach house fronting a cobblestoned courtyard.

Some photographers prefer to work within the confines of their studios, where they have total control of the light and are free from dependence on the weather. Early in his career one prominent photographer would shoot models on his roof against seamless paper. "Today," he says, "I like to control all elements. Working outside is unpleasant because so many buildings have made New York darker and darker." He adds, "If I work outside, I want it to be on a fabulous island with a wonderful house and servants."

Although studios vary in size and amenities provided (supersuccessful Mike Reinhardt has a sauna in his spacious studio-cum-living space), most have a room that doubles as recreation area and office; a kitchen; a dressing room where the models change; and a darkroom where developing and printing are done. Studio walls are painted white to prevent any color reflecting on the model, and, ideally, there is a skylight or huge window to provide natural light. Rolls of seamless paper in various colors are used as backdrops, with black, white, and gray the most popular. Some photographers simulate actual sites by constructing environments in their studio; others, like Scavullo and Avedon, prefer to shoot against the paper. If there is enough space, a photographer may keep tables, chairs, and screens on hand and rent additional props.

Basic studio equipment includes electronic lighting units balanced to simulate daylight and outfitted with various reflectors plus spotlights for highlighting and backlighting. If a shot is to be hard edged and direct, the photographer can emphasize shadows and lines with a strong light from above the model. Indirect or diffused lighting, created by "bouncing" light off a white wall or covering a lens with gauze, produces a softer, more romantic effect. The photographer's arsenal of equipment also includes assorted camera bodies, interchangeable lenses, and attachments for close-ups or distant shots. Motorized thirty-five-millimeter cameras that produce four pictures per second are popular for capturing the subtle gradations of a model's expression. Alberto Rizzo admits that he, like so many other photographers, owns too many cameras. "All I really need is a camera body with a fifty-millimeter lens approximating the way the eye sees," he admits.

For some adventurous photographers a location assignment can be a welcome change. If the spot is idyllic, a shoot can have the festive air of a holiday outing. The photographer, assistants, and fellow travelers (friends of the client, account executives, copywriters, agency assistants, an art director, and associate art directors) pile in a van filled with valuable equipment, props, reflector cards, film, an exposure meter, clothes and accessories, and head out to Jones Beach or an abandoned railroad in New Jersey. Sometimes a site in the center of the city may be more suitable; a bridle path in Central Park, the Metropolitan Museum of Art's imposing facade, or the Cloisters are frequent backdrops.

One- or two-week bookings at magical sites around the world can be particularly exciting. Although most shootings proceed without mishap, foreign environments are less than predictable. Generally extra time is needed to scout locations and work around changing weather conditions.

Model Jane Hundley leaving a photographer's studio—the case contains
the makeup and accessories that she carries to every shoot.

But the adaptable professional can work under adverse conditions and make virtue out of defects.

A photographer is plagued with constant fears: bored customs officials might delay the shooting for days by confiscating equipment; a complicated strobe hookup might malfunction; models may develop sun or food poisoning, be unable to hold a pose because of a swarm of flies, or have claimed to be expert sportswomen when in fact they can't swim, ski, or sail. Or he may discover that his fabulous concept isn't working out pictorially; reality doesn't coincide with the image he has in his mind; or initial darkroom work reveals that color film is turning out green. But when the pictures are successful, the time, effort, and expenditure are more than worthwhile.

When Cacharel first designed men's clothes, Art Kane, a brilliant and inventive photographer famed for his color work, was flown to Paris to discuss the new line. Having been an art director for eleven years, Kane was given the very rare freedom to create the concepts for Cacharel. Because Sarah Moon had photographed Cacharel's women's clothes in a soft-focused, romantic way, Kane decided that his images would be strong and dynamic. Stimulated by Hitchcock's memorable *North by Northwest,* he sketched a number of ideas that revolved around a man pursued by an airplane. At the site, Antelope Valley in the California desert, he told the model, Ingo, to flee from a plane chasing him (incidentally the same one used in Hitchcock's film). Kane prefers location shooting because he never knows what might happen—"It can be something incredible! There's always the unexpected—the unpredictable!"

Distinctive effects can be achieved in a studio, too. An hour before a studio shooting begins, the model arrives to have her hair, face, and clothing styled. Unless they are carefully constructed in the best fabrics, outfits that appear in ads or editorials rarely look as attractive on a customer as they do on a model—and for good reason. A stylist (or an editor for a fashion story) uses every possible device to enhance the clothes. Because the model is photographed with her back against seamless paper, the stylist may pin, tape, or cut the back of the clothes; she might put weights on the bottoms of trousers or stuff the back to improve the fit, and she sometimes twists, drapes, or even wets a jacket to give it a casual, lived-in feeling.

Albert Rizzo (photographer): "Guy Bourdin is admired by everyone; they think all they have to do is copy his style. They don't realize they must lead his style of life to get his style."

No matter how much experience a stylist has had, each session entails a slightly different approach. Once, when photographer Arthur Elgort asked the models to move around a furniture-filled set, Kezia Keeble had to make sure that none of her temporary alterations would show in the pictures.

The efforts of hair and makeup artists can mean the difference between a model looking attractive or ravishing. Mark Pipino, coowner of the Pipino-Buccheri beauty salon in New York City, does free-lance styling on ads and editorials. Before he creates a hairdo for a shot, he discusses the clothes with the editor or photographer; if the collar is the focal point, Pipino might provide a rolled, upswept style influenced by the last Paris collection or perhaps by a woman strolling down the street. Pipino's soft-spoken manner is invaluable in putting a model at ease and dissipating the tension built into an important booking.

In a fashion shot makeup is as important as clothes and hair. The kind of lighting the photographer will use dictates how heavily cosmetics are applied; for a black-and-white photo more intense contrast is needed to emphasize the model's facial planes. Pierre Larouche, an innovative free-lance makeup artist, believes that "makeup should not follow a pattern; instead each maquillage should transfigure, as well as reveal, a woman's uniqueness." Way Bandy, another outstanding free-lance makeup expert and author, observed in *W*, "a trend toward elimination rather than accumulation . . . a face colored so naturally that the artifice is there, but not seen. The effect is one of honest, healthy, natural good looks." A makeup artist, like a painter working on a clean canvas, uses color to blend, brush, outline, dab, highlight, and disguise. The finished product is a confident beauty ready to face the camera.

Just before the shoot a young, underpaid assistant will set up the tripod, load the camera, attach the appropriate lens, and position the lights; most photographers prefer male assistants because of the necessity of transporting heavy equipment and constructing sets. Now the model emerges, and Polaroid shots are taken as a guide to balancing the illumination of foreground and background. If the photographer senses that she is nervous, he uses one of several methods to relax her. He may show her the Polaroids before the actual shots are taken; chat with her and explain the effect he wants; put screens around her to conjure a feeling of intimacy; suggest a story that will evoke an appropriate response; assure her that she is the most spectacular beauty that has ever walked into the studio; and treat her like a fragile prima donna. If personal problems or a model's inability to follow instructions destroy the realization of his concept, the photographer creates a different situation in order to elicit the exchange of feelings essential to produce a successful picture.

For Robert Farber the best shooting situation occurs "when a model and photographer are attuned to each other's mood. It's like a short-lived romance; a mutual feeling develops, and in that situation words are un-

necessary." Although Klaus Lucka avoids personal involvement with his models, he admits, "Flirting is one of the great things in life, although the moment you have the first bite, you lose your appetite."

Avedon elicits the intensity of thoroughbred horses from the women he photographs. According to former model China Machado, "More was not enough. I'd do the most incredible things with my body for Avedon in front of the camera. But when I tried to do them at home in front of the mirror, I couldn't."

Energetic perfectionist Mike Reinhardt feels that a close emotional rapport with a model has produced some of his strongest pictures, especially those of Janice Dickenson, a top model whom he photographs and lives with.

Male photographers tend to cajole or coerce, while female photographers are more likely to explain the motivation behind the picture. Jean

Pagliuso will tell a model not to expect any verbal reinforcement. "Not only would excessive flattery sound artificial," she explains, "but models are professional and narcissistic enough to work without reinforcement."

Although some photographers work in silence or play classical music, most prefer a disco sound to create a lively atmosphere; Skrebneski admitted to a journalist, "The beat drives me insane, but the models love it."

Whether an assignment is shot on location or in a studio, it isn't complete until black-and-white contact sheets or color slides have been developed, sorted, and delivered to the client or editor, who, ninety-nine percent of the time, makes the final selection.

Commercial concerns can inhibit creativity. Sometimes a financially successful photographer is so distressed by the thought of shooting another product for a timid art director that he may switch his base of operations to London, Paris, or Milan. Although Europe is notorious for lower pay and limited equipment, many Americans welcome the chance to enter a market where the photographer is a star and greater fashion awareness guides advertisers and editors.

Because the European audience is smaller, the emphasis is more on attitude than merchandise. With less responsibility to the advertiser, a photographer can create erotic or ambiguous pictures that emphasize a situation, rather than a product, and may even hide a portion of the clothing. Italian *Bazaar* pays approximately $50 a page, a small sum compared to U.S. fees, but accords the photographer tremendous freedom. He is simply given the clothes, told where to go, and instructed to bring back ten moody, sensuous shots—shots that he knows won't be arbitrarily cropped. Working in Europe has other aesthetic compensations: a larger format and higher quality paper in the magazines, plus the possibility of creating a portfolio of experimental work. But photographers accustomed to a more extravagant life-style often return to New York, where the money is.

There is a certain amount of freedom, too, for the highly talented photographer. As a photography critic wrote, "Fashion photography is disbelief made graphic." Some make it more graphic than others, and as time passes, different approaches are used to nourish the fantasies of the fashion conscious.

In the 1920s photographers posed models with serene expressions in highly controlled settings with classic statuary as props; the emphasis was on purity of line. Photography was confined to studios, because the large-format cameras then in use were too heavy to carry on location; film was too slow to adjust to changes in outdoor light; and the portable strobe unit had not been invented. In the 1930s and 1940s static pictures of icy, ethereal creatures in couture clothes prevailed. A few photographers did experiment. In the 1930s Martin Munkacsi shot many exceptional exterior photos for *Harper's Bazaar.* His models were often shown in motion,

---

Barbara Rose (art critic, on Helmut Newton's latest book, *Sleepless Nights,* in *Vogue*): "In Newton's photos, the objects are as real as the people, the people as highly polished and perfectly formed as their environment. Newton combines the opulence and luxury of French taste for beautiful surfaces with a German eye for psychologically revealing observations that define the spirit of a time."

---

demonstrating Munkacsi's preference for the real world rather than the hothouse studio fantasies of Baron de Meyer, Beaton, Horst, and Hoyningen-Huene. Because photography was never restricted by the sexist taboos associated with painting and sculpture, in the 1940s and 1950s women like Toni Frissell and Louise Dahl-Wolfe were able to pursue successful careers in photography.

In 1947, twenty-four-year-old Richard Avedon, who admired Munkacsi's spontaneity, set fashion photography on its heels. Commissioned by *Harper's Bazaar,* he worked tirelessly to create new angles and use unusual locations. He democratized fashion photography and injected a sense of fun when he put spectacular models in fabulous haute couture on roller skates and in working-class bars. In 1955, he created one of his most arresting images: Dovima surrounded by elephants at the Cirque d'Hiver.

Avedon's style is sleek, fast, and chic; he is still intensely dedicated to his art. To keep the viewer's attention totally on the model, he usually shoots them against white seamless paper. He may pull some sixty prints until he gets the perfect picture. Truman Capote's introduction to Avedon's 1959 *Observations* sums up the photographer's work: "Avedon finds his proper tongue in silence, and while maneuvering a camera, his voice, the one that speaks with admirable clarity, is the soft sound of the shutter forever freezing a moment focused by his precision." Avedon is the only photographer apotheosized by the Metropolitan Museum of Art with a one-man exhibition, held in 1978.

Until the 1960s the fashion field was dominated by Avedon and Irving Penn, who photographed models as if they were still lifes and produced stylized images of breathtaking clarity. After World War II the development of the small, lightweight thirty-five-millimeter camera with its fast lenses offered more freedom; no longer an encumbrance the camera became an extension of the photographer's eye. The invention of the strobe unit made it possible to create the same daylight effects as tungsten without generating as much heat.

When Penn and Avedon were in their prime, they had a number of advantages not available to contemporary photographers. Because fashion magazines had fewer readers, it was easier to develop an individual philosophy and execute innovative ideas. Instead of considering an enormous audience and the needs of advertisers, photographers had ideal working situations and enough time to develop an identifiable point of view; an editor-in-chief was more likely to collaborate in creating a unique look.

Today few photographers have a strong signature. Scavullo is one of

them: an extraordinary lighting technique has made his portraits of flaw-less beauties readily identifiable as his work.

Chris Von Wangenheim's photos are sophisticated, sexy, and ambigu-ous; the viewer supplies an explanation for the situation displayed. Von Wangenheim, who emigrated from Germany in 1965, has been accused of capitalizing on decadence and violence. The implication of such accusa-tions is that he has no right to report or interpret cultural trends, some-thing he does with tremendous style.

In Europe photographers are never accused of being too erotic or per-verse; what is important there is the impact of an image. England's David Bailey and Italy's Toscani are respected for their originality. Deborah Turbeville, an American whose desire for a more artistic environment motivated her to set up a studio in Paris, will spend a day producing one dreamlike photo of elusive models posed, off-center, in empty rooms, fac-tories, or forests. She, Newton, and Guy Bourdin seem to be inspired by movies and forbidden fantasies to produce exquisite imagery; their young models pose in an overtly sexual way or convey a detached kind of eroti-cism.

Helmut Newton's brilliant photographs portray recurrent themes. Most often stunning women enact sado-masochistic dramas; their intima-cy is a far cry from the style of the 1960s, when models like Twiggy, Ver-ushka, and Marisa Berenson stood in isolated splendor. Newton's heroines pose in overly rich, claustrophobic surroundings, cringe against skyscraper windows, or are pursued by dogs; the results are stunning and unsettling.

If imitation is the sincerest form of flattery, Guy Bourdin can feel flat-tered. Regarded by his contemporaries as the most experimental image maker working today, he is one of the few photographers who do not re-peat a successful idea but constantly try new concepts. Bourdin's beauti-fully composed, dramatic pictures spark French *Vogue*'s editorial pages, and his mysterious, atmospheric ads for Charles Jourdan represent a new high in advertising.

Whether a photographer works in Europe or America, the psychologi-cal rewards are similar. Says one successful photographer, "The greatest satisfaction occurs when I can say no to a really awful job, if the client wants something that is too contrary to what I want to do." Art Kane's pleasure lies in "realizing my fantasies—and seeing them pub-lished." Yet another photographer loves "the glamour, the excitement of each new day spent with another beautiful woman."

Some of its foremost practitioners complain that fashion photography is irreverent, romantic escapism—nothing more than a glittering, glamorous facade. But as long as women believe that their lives will be enhanced by buying products shown in fashion magazines, photographers will continue to exert an enormous influence by depicting the stuff of dreams.

CHAPTER SEVEN

THE PRESS

FASHION COVERAGE IS MORE THAN A NINE-TO-FIVE JOB

> "Today's woman knows that to be in fashion is to look like an extension of her mind, self, and body—that it is the woman who makes the clothes—not the other way around."
>
> —Carrie Donovan, *The New York Times Magazine*

A pyrotechnic shower of bronze and apricot . . . a floating nightsky of a dress . . . blossoming organza appliqués . . . aubergine and pearls before midnight. Who can resist the fashion writer's sequined syllables and the sensuous photography found only in the fashion press? Even if a spellbound reader cannot afford the clothes splashed across those glossy pages, the glamour is still hers—vicariously. Her favorite magazines encourage her to play roles, to explore, to discover who she is and who she would like to be. And the money she spends along the way is hardly incidental.

Thousands of fashion-oriented women are enticed by the promises, by the expectations that these publications raise with their provocative suggestions. "Why is November so dazzzzlingly different?" a *Vogue* editorial asks. "The quick, unexpected turn that's the difference between dazzle and dazzzzle," it replies; then tells the breathless readers what feels right this month. The fashion press is in the business of making women dissatisfied with the serviceable wardrobes they currently own. Without their constant suggestions to add seamed stockings, a strapless suede top, or a mohair coat, the fashion industry would wither like a vineyard in a drought. Fashion editorials act as a seal of approval for thousands of women, a number of whom study a picture down to its painstakingly selected accessories and purchase the entire outfit because they feel too insecure to make their own choices. A clear drawback to this approach is that many customers lack the proportions or the attitude to carry dramatic silhouettes; they are dwarfed rather than enhanced by certain designers' clothes.

Nevertheless the industry continues to produce expensive and eccentric fashions, and the press continues to promote them. As designers turn

Diana Vreeland, doyenne of the fashion world, and leading model Jerry Hall.

their attention from one erogenous zone to another (thighs, breasts, ankles, waist), sound business practice dictates that the magazines follow. Like loving and selfless handmaidens, they applaud each "new" vision—the mini, the midi, the A-line, the layered look—with a cornucopia of superlatives otherwise reserved for the treasures in a boy-king's excavated tomb.

Although the American publications are visually appealing and enjoyable to skim through, that element of surprise found in European fashion magazines is rarely evident on their pages. With exceptions, like Deborah Turbeville's controversial soft-focused photos of beautiful, isolated women in a New York steam bath, few American editorial spreads are startling or masterful. In order to survive, the American magazines must cater to the conservative advertisers scattered across the country who support them (*Vogue* editors admit to the existence of the "must list" of big advertisers whose clothes "must" appear on the editorial pages.) When the cost of paper, binding, and distribution rose, American periodicals responded by using smaller-sized, less expensive paper and increasing the number of advertisements; the European magazines preferred to raise their prices in order to retain a high-quality stock and larger format.

American fashion magazines were much more stimulating in the days when brilliant art directors like the strong-willed White Russian Alexey Brodovitch and dedicated editors-in-chief like Carmel Snow, both of *Harper's Bazaar,* spent endless hours choosing photos that emphasized a power and beauty that most readers could rarely attain; gorgeous eclectic images, never arbitrarily cropped and printed on large-format paper, made turning pages an endless source of fantasy and delight. And *Vogue* under Diana Vreeland from 1963 to 1971 was filled with stylized, fantasy-oriented images. Describing his reactions to the great fashion magazines, Yves St. Laurent wrote in a preface to Nancy Hall Duncan's *History of Fashion Photography,* "I see myself once more. I am very young. Feverishly I wait each month for them . . . From their satin paper, I receive ripples of passion . . ."

But the days are long gone when flamboyant and imperious editors, like Eve Arden in *Funny Face,* Hollywood's romanticized view of the fash-

---

Jeff Schwager (VP of D. D. Dominick): "I regard the press as the fashion Mafia. While some editors are excellent, others don't know what fashion is about. They cover up their lack of knowledge with well-worn phrases, like 'Isn't it chic?' or 'Isn't it fabulous?'"

Richard Bernstein (artist): "*Vogue* and *Bazaar* concentrate on established designers who advertise."

ion world, shouted orders to their underlings. Today a more realistic sensibility has taken over. Instead of concentrating on producing glorious images, emphasis is placed on reaching readers whose preferences are requested in monthly polls that affect editorial decisions. The readers of the 1980s are liberated, active, and career minded. Along with suggestions on how to look better than ever, they demand information about beauty products, exercise, vitamins, nutrition, and special diets. And all of it must be packaged in a fast-paced format with quick headlines that gallop across the page. The strength of a magazine depends on editors who can balance financial realities with aesthetic concerns—and, at the same time, project the intangible quality that creates a distinctive look.

America's most prestigious fashion magazines are *Vogue* and *Harper's Bazaar*. *Vogue*'s 1,007,513 readers are affluent and sophisticated. At a median age of 32.4 years they are concerned with a total life-style: theater, film, art, books, interiors, travel, celebrity interviews. With a circulation of 550,000 *Bazaar* is directed to a more specific audience: the successful executive woman who wants career advice as well as beauty and fashion hints. While these publications cater to upper-income fashionables, *Glamour* and *Mademoiselle* focus on a younger college- or career-oriented market. *Seventeen,* which has no competition, attracts an ever younger audience: thirteen- to nineteen-year-olds. Other women's magazines offer limited fashion coverage. Geared to a single life-style, *Cosmopolitan* has enormous fashion impact on its receptive readers; one cover featuring a seductive model in a Kamali swimsuit had young women across the country clamoring for the garment.

In contrast there are very few American men's fashion magazines. One reason is that heterosexual men do not respond easily to the good looks of male models. With the exception of a homosexual minority of sartorial pacesetters, the male population is noted for a barely developed fashion consciousness. Most will refurbish their wardrobes with similar kinds of clothes: unimaginatively cut dark suits; made-to-order shirts (if they can afford them); jeans; classic sweaters; and a trench coat with a zip-out lining. There are indications that this pattern is changing, however. Because of the increase in designer clothes made for men, the American male seems to be exercising his aesthetic sensibility, appreciating quality and good design, and choosing clothes that are stylish as well as functional.

Trade newspapers and newspaper fashion editorials are as important to the fashion industry as the consumer magazines. Although John Fairchild publishes fifteen trade papers on subjects as diverse as men's wear, electronics, footwear, and metallurgy, *Women's Wear Daily* is his most influential. It is considered the Bible by some and the scourge by others, depending on how favorably and frequently they've been covered in its pages. *New York* magazine has described it as "the publication that rules the fashion and society worlds with a whim of iron." The cream of the international press is front and center at European and American collections, but only *WWD* can inform its seventy-five thousand subscribers almost immediately that, "Trim crisp suits take shape . . . A big trend on Seventh Avenue as well as the Paris couture."

Women's Wear picks up a look quickly and documents it with consistently high-quality photographs or illustrations. Like doctors on call, its sharp-eyed photographers carry beepers. When they're informed of exactly where the action is and arrive at a fashion show or party, they are automatically given first-class treatment. *WWD* is far more than a trade paper reporting news; it creates trends by labeling them (high chic, low chic, serious chic), enshrining them on the front cover, and displaying the BYP (beautiful young people) and the BOP (beautiful older people) dressed in whatever it's promoting that day. Special issues focus on different areas of the industry—furs, accessories, lingerie, children's apparel, swimwear—and highlight the best in each category. As one designer complained, "If *WWD* doesn't mention you, you don't exist; it is sad but true that most of the fashion industry looks to *WWD* for direction and is too conservative to think for itself."

Because of its personal glimpses of fashion movers in action and designers at work, *Women's Wear* is habit-forming. Whether or not they admit it, buyers, publicists, merchandisers, and designers first turn to its acidic, gossip-filled "Eye" column to see who wore what to where, what was said, and why they weren't invited to a social event in Dallas, Washington, D.C., New York, London, Paris, or Milan. To its credit the paper is also a reliable source for such pertinent information as buyers' arrivals, company profits, executive changes, job offerings, art reviews, and interviews.

Edith Locke: "*WWD* is *WWD*; it's its own little world; a trade publication read by all those interested in fashion. But as a fashion/beauty magazine we must rely on our own convictions."

Jerry Hall with Andy Warhol at a party celebrating *Interview* magazine.

Ralph Lauren: "The press looks at clothes in terms of newness, a statement—something they can get their teeth into and do editorials about. Sometimes when the press thinks you're fabulous, consumers aren't interested."

W, another Fairchild publication, is directed to consumers rather than fashion-industry insiders, though trendsetters do read both. A biweekly with a larger format than *Women's Wear Daily,* it shows the best of the designer collections in glowing color. Moreover its one hundred eighty thousand readers are treated to crisp interviews (often reprinted from *WWD*) with newsworthy fashion, art, and literary figures and extensive coverage of designers' life-styles. One finds flattering photographs of world traveler Giorgio Sant'Angelo relaxing in his exquisite artifact-filled Park Avenue apartment; Betsey Johnson in her all-pink SoHo loft; health addict Bill Kaiserman in his Beekman Terrace townhouse featuring walls covered with thirty coats of paint to simulate a faded Portofino villa; the regal Pauline Trigère with her collection of some six hundred turtles (symbols of good luck and longevity); Diane Von Furstenberg reclining on a $12,000 custom-made satin-tufted bed in her palatial Fifth Avenue apartment; Mary McFadden in her treasure-filled showroom. Still its main focus is fashion. Eager for news of the latest designs and all those marvelous parties filled with the powerful and the beautiful, the style-conscious readers devour its pages. In *W* they get fashion scoops without having to wade through trade items relevant only to the industry.

Direction for *W* comes from John Fairchild, a powerful figure who has maintained his number-one position in the fashion press with a fresh, aggressive point of view. But a publisher is only as effective as his employees. Fairchild has assembled a staff able to withstand daily deadline pressures and determine what's most timely.

Etta Froio, fashion editor of both *WWD* and *W,* is unknown to the clothes-buying public. A capable, attractive woman who does her demanding job with modesty and quiet assurance, Froio is always on top of what's happening in the fashion world. In constant touch with the publications' bureaus around the world, she plans special features, reviews designer collections, and edits copy. In defense of *WWD*'s trend-setting policies, she says, "*WWD* doesn't create fashion, but reflects and presents it in an exciting way—covering as many collections as possible and without letting personal feelings affect that reporting. . . . I see certain designers socially," Froio admits, "but I can't allow it to affect my job. When

I covered sportswear, I had to review a friend's collection. I reported it objectively—and we've never had the same close relationship again. A personal relationship can be dangerous if it affects the way you do your job."

Most editors are unwilling to criticize the fashion industry. A notable exception is Phyllis Tweel, formerly with the *Daily News Record,* Fairchild Publications' men's wear paper and now a gossip columnist for the style-conscious *SoHo Weekly News.* Her quicksilver takes on the fashion world, her puns, put downs and incisive interviews, make her work a perfect antidote to the overinflated fashion prose now prevalent. Publicist Roz Rubenstein describes Tweel as "on the beam—the gossip queen of New York and, right or wrong, without fear." Tweel's light, satirical column in *DNR,* "Between the Lines," reported on fashion and social events; her reviews occasionally bordered on verbal execution of certain fashion luminaries. Tweel admits that her audience "loves what I write—until I write about them." After she published some scathing observations on a certain designer's line, for example, he molested her so seriously that she was treated at a hospital.

Tweel's personal style is as vibrant as her writing style. A fashion original, she wore anklets with high heels two years before they were fashionable and bought Karl Lagerfeld's highly constructed coats before he was a top couturier. These days her work uniform tends to be one of Norma Kamali's head-spinning clinging dresses.

The *New York Post*'s Eugenia Sheppard, one of America's most renowned fashion columnists, operates in a very different vein. In eighty papers across the country readers who aspire to more glamorous lives follow the activities of the fashionables whom Eugenia made famous. Their faces appear and reappear, photographed at parties and fashion shows, somehow retaining their radiant beauty year after year after year. Her influence is such that just by frequently mentioning a designer's name in reports of fashion shows, balls, and dinners, she can build his image, make him a household word, and increase sales of his scarves, hats, home furnishings, blouses, belts, shoes, handbags, and perfume. During a

John Molloy (author of *Dress for Success*): "Fashion is a monolithic tyranny consisting of the fashion industry and its satellites, the fashion publications who set out to defraud the customer by forcing her to buy clothes that are destined to be discarded after a season or two."

conversation taped for *Interview* magazine, Paulette Goddard told Eugenia, "You have a very special quality that's characteristic of great artists . . . You see everything for the first time. I see you at fashion shows, for instance, and you're looking at every detail with complete enthusiasm while others are dozing off."

Aileen Mehle, or "Suzy," is another influential journalist. Her gossip column, which appears in the New York *Daily News* and is syndicated in eighty-nine newspapers, fulfills an unquenchably curious public that wants to know exactly what Pauline Trigère served for dessert. Suzy's success lies in writing about whom the fashionables are marrying, divorcing, and dining with.

Fashion fanatics can never get enough of the latest trends. To keep them informed, Andy Warhol's *Interview* magazine devotes itself to documenting the frenetic pace of international doers. Unlike publications that dispense revelations, service pieces, or news analyses, *Interview* gives its approximately one hundred thousand readers in New York, Los Angeles, London, Rome, and Paris "conversations" (with nothing left out) with the stars of yesterday, today, and tomorrow. Moreover there are photographs of the beautiful and rich (preferably people who are both) and those, such as George Willig, who scaled the World Trade Center, who have been famous for fifteen minutes.

Although *Interview* ostensibly covers art, entertainment, fashion, and society, it thrives on semi-intimate, amusing small talk. Often its interviews are conducted between two ultrafashionable celebrities who are known not for their journalistic expertise but for success in such fields as design or entertainment. For example, when *Interview* sent Bianca Jagger to interview impressionable young Jack Ford at the White House, circulation for that month jumped ten thousand. Other noteworthy issues featured J. Paul Getty III (of kidnapping fame) chatting with writer William Burroughs and the imperturbable Halston, who not only "dressed author Lally Weymouth for lunch" but plied her with light-hearted questions.

Interview is a voyeur's delight, specializing in delectable young princes and princesses, rock divas, avant-garde designers, and film luminaries, all of them exuding an air of glamour and ennui. Typical articles feature conversations with the rejuvenated Truman Capote or talented Tony Perkins, and pieces on Bianca Jagger's plans for the future or Elsa Peretti's idyllic "farmhouse" outside Barcelona. Incisive editor Bob Colachello (who rarely registers surprise) once reported that Marisa Berenson "leaned into a candle while trying to take a close look at—some words are best not

Jewelry designer Elsa Peretti and *Interview* magazine's business manager, Fred Hughes, strike a fashionable pose.

written. Her hairdo burst into flames, and her gallant date bravely extinguished the conflagration—with Perrier, naturellement."

Interview's specialty is handsome design and page after page of the sexiest people in town. "I'm one of their greatest fans," a film maker admits. "Whenever I can't reach my friends via phone, I can always see what they're up to on the pages of *Interview*—especially in Colachello's 'Out' column. I feel very close to the magazine. There's a kind of magic to it." Another reader describes *Interview* as "graphically brilliant, but occasionally lacking in real content—a perfect publication for illiterates and foreigners who don't speak English."

Richard Bernstein, *Interview*'s cover designer, feels that the magazine has charisma because, "Warhol has a huge following dating back to the sixties who relate to his films and art. Andy is one of America's contemporary kingpins, symbol of the avant-garde. His suggestions permeate every issue."

The newsprint magazine is produced on an enormous floor filled with Art Deco (Warhol is a passionate collector of pieces from the period) on Broadway at the corner of Union Square. At any time of day Warhol may be photographing Bianca Jagger, working on one of his many silk screen/acrylic portraits of Halston, Nan Kempner, or Liz Taylor Warner, or having lunch with a half-dozen glitterati. Occasionally it is possible to reach Colachello, who is out more often than not. In between trips to Cartagena or tête-à-têtes with the Concorde set, Colachello manages to keep Warhol posted on upcoming projects.

Colachello's satisfaction comes from saturating the pages with star-potential figures: "For example, as a result of one interview, Linda Hutton—Lauren's younger sister—received many modeling offers." He adds, "What we're interested in is shock-value stories. We know the fashion and film industries watch us. Magazines like *Time* and *Newsweek* often borrow gossip items and photos from us."

Asked why so many celebrities enjoy interviewing, and, more important, being interviewed, Colachello explains, "We are in a unique position because of Andy Warhol—the favorite of the art crowd and cognoscenti. As the most-written-about artist in the world he really understands celeb-

Edith Locke (Editor-in chief of *Mademoiselle*): "Some editors look terrific and have learned what suits them. Some newspaper people don't and should! When someone photographs clothes and chooses accessories, something should rub off."

A highly successful fashion photographer: "I don't go to fashion shows; I can see the edited clothes in *W*."

rities. He already knows all the standard angles because he's been subjected to and can get past the usual run-of-the-mill questions. He can speak more freely to the stars, who are also his friends. In fact people like Liza [Minnelli] and Raquel [Welch] have given their best interviews to Andy, probably because they feel so relaxed talking to him. They don't consider him a journalist—they consider him another celebrity."

Night is a monthly picture newspaper published by videomaker Anton Perich, who also photographs the style setters at their favorite discos who flirt outrageously when they're not whirling deliriously across the dance floors. *Night* also features fragmentary interviews. When asked for his earliest childhood remembrance, for example, Prince Egon Von Furstenberg replied, "Wearing a baby-blue taffeta blouse. I was two."

Without the fashion press to report the latest trends and gossip, more than a little glamour would disappear from our lives. And without the fashion editor none of these publications could exist. Contrary to the myths perpetuated in Hollywood movies, a fashion editor does more than deliver directives to a sheeplike audience, enjoy leisurely lunches with charming designers, and supervise shootings in exotic parts of the world. There is considerable frustration and hard work along with the excitement. She views endless collections but never has sufficient time in which to see everything; she sometimes supports a line only to discover that the manufacturer cannot produce the clothes for which she's generated demand. She is besieged by publicists and designers seeking coverage and by models and photographers seeking work. Aware that any repackaging of the body must be perfectly timed for when an issue hits the stands three months from its inception, she sifts out trends and serves them up in the most palatable form possible.

In a nonstop search for the newest direction, editors, like buyers, work eighteen hours per day in an atmosphere of competitive hysteria to cover the European and New York collections. Ceaselessly packing and unpacking, they do the European circuit first. Unlike New York designers, whose showings are usually held within a compact area on or about Seventh Avenue, the Europeans outdo themselves by selecting increasingly outrageous locations each season (the press still talks about a prêt-à-porter—ready-to-wear—show in the sewers of Paris). As St. Laurent confided to *W*, "The current system of ready-to-wear shows, with their theatrics, is

simply abominable. It used to be great to see the prêt-à-porter and its impact. Now it's close to a nightmare with all the attention given to sensationalism."

Accompanied by photographers weighted down by heavy equipment, the editors undertake the complex logistical planning involved in attending some ninety-two shows. While everyone battles to get into the most popular ones, those with top fashion press credentials are assured entrance. Their minds click away like computers as they absorb details, appraise new fabrics, and perpetually take notes. Hailing those hard-to-find taxis as they zoom from show to show, they're constantly running into other chain-smoking, sharp-eyed editors who manage—heaven knows how—not to collapse from exhaustion. As the days pass, the standard fashion greeting—"Darling, you look fabulous!" followed by a barely perceptible kiss on both cheeks—diminishes in intensity.

The press realizes that the best fashion shows often take place on the street. A canny editor will observe that the chic women of Paris are already wearing the looks just previewed on the runways. Others are totally original: an Edith Piaf look-alike saunters by in a glittering chiffon scarf and a tough World War II leather coat; a student stops traffic in ruby-red cowboy boots and thigh-high silk hose with hand-embroidered hearts. The street is a striking laboratory where the young experiment, and many of the designers reap the results. And all along, the editor must anticipate what will be coming.

After seeing ten shows daily for ten days—fighting over seats, trying to see past blinding flashbulbs, listening to other opinionated journalists who can't imagine being wrong—the editors' vision blurs and their circuits overload. Nevertheless they are already en route to New York for yet another round of fashion shows.

Meanwhile each editor is also planning eye-catching new editorials. Even if a designer isn't making an earth-shattering statement with a new collection, an editor can create fashion excitement by having the clothes photographed in dramatic locations (the World Trade Center, disco palaces, the West Side Highway) with distinctive accessories, like crystal-drop earrings, a marabou fan, multihued suede pumps.

Once she's determined her subject, the editor is responsible for engineering a successful shooting session. Although the components vary, a typical shoot might unfold as follows. In a cavernous Fifth Avenue photographer's studio, the remains of a take-out Chinese banquet from a nearby restaurant litter a huge table. A model sits before a brightly lit makeup mirror. A free-lance hair stylist like John Sahag (who commutes

WWD's senior vice-president, Michael Coady, and fashion editor Etta Froio, after a round of shows at 550 Seventh Avenue, one of New York fashion's most pretigious addresses.

Mort Scheinman (*WWD*'s managing editor): "Advertisers do not receive the preferential treatment that certain fashion magazines offer them. Our advertising sales people aren't permitted contact with the editors—they aren't even allowed on the editorial floor."

from New York to Paris every other month, earns $750 to $1,000 a day on advertising assignments, and also works for prestigious fashion magazines for that invaluable credit line and fees that he blithely calls "taxi fare") is using a curling iron to give her the latest look. Two of the French photographer's assistants adjust the lights and reload the camera. A makeup artist sits quietly drinking orange juice while waiting to work on the next model. Meanwhile the editor is rummaging through the extensive accessory collection she has brought for a pair of mauve stiletto heels and a narrow white belt. She decides that curved gold earrings will best enhance the St. Laurent suit that's the subject of this shot.

Pleased with the new rolled hairdo Sahag has miraculously created within minutes, the model is now ready to work. Somewhat skittishly she moves across a white set bounded by enormous white screens that throw highlights onto her face. An assistant editor plays the latest disco record; its pulsating, repetitive beat engulfs the loft.

"Move! Move like a black girl in Harlem!" shouts the photographer, and the model responds with greater confidence. "Come on . . . Beautiful! You look terrific. Like that! Move! Move! Like that. Perfect!"

The atmosphere intensifies as a razor-sharp rapport builds between model and photographer. The editor watches. Alert to every nuance, aware of which details to emphasize, she requests a momentary pause to adjust the collar, switch earrings, and tighten the belt. "Roll up the sleeves of the jacket! Use the pockets," she instructs the model. At the same time Sahag brushes out the model's hair in sure, rapid strokes, then turns on the wind machine to create a natural look.

The model begins to strut and pivot. Displaying an electrifying smile, she hits her peak: she's a gorgeous, glowing, all-American beauty.

"All right. Good." The photographer takes a much needed break. His assistant dims the lights, and the model leaves.

A second model arrives. Kisses and warm greetings are exchanged. The photographer devotes sixty seconds to massaging her shoulders before a similar scenario begins, ending when eight garments have been perfectly accessorized and captured on film. Throughout it all the editor has maintained an amazing calm.

Although it is easier to work in the controlled atmosphere of a photographer's studio, editors often go on location to add the flavor of an exotic environment to their fashion stories; moreover it is essential to shoot beachwear in winter in order to have pictures ready in time for summer issues. Despite the fact that the background is rarely emphasized in contemporary fashion shots, the editor and photographer spend a day or two scouting for the most impressive sites. The editor informs him of how many pictures are required and what kind of clothes will be shot and trusts that he will do a competent and, perhaps, even a distinctive job. She selects the most suitable accessories in the magazine's stock of props and packs more clothes and accessories than are actually needed. "You'll never know how they look till you see them on location" is conventional editorial wisdom.

One well-known fashion photographer who does extensive location shooting points out that, "An airline will often provide free transportation for the photographer, assistants, models, editor, and hair and make-up stylists in return for publication of a photo of them boarding the plane." Still fees, hotels, and meals for the staff make a trip to Tobago, Tivoli, or Thailand very costly. Dealing with the exigencies of a location shoot makes it imperative for an editor to choose a reliable photographer whose style matches the mood desired for a story. For example, Chris Von Wangenheim can produce detached-looking models in a cool, erotic atmosphere, while Mike Reinhardt might be booked for pictures of energetic women exuding a glowing vitality.

When they arrive at their location, the editor arranges hotel accommodations and meals for the crew. Acting as den mother ("If I had children, I'd like to think they'd be better behaved," complains one editor), she keeps her charges under control while she worries about the clothes' prompt arrival and passage through customs and ensures that they are handled carefully; they will have to be returned to the manufacturer. And she is always concerned about the weather. If the photographer prefers the diffused light of early morning, it is her responsibility to awaken the models at 5:00 A.M. to have their faces made up and hair done so they will be ready to work when called. If no stylist is available, the editor presses the clothes and spends the day pinning, tucking, accessorizing, and overseeing. She might suggest that the models move in a certain way to

Bill Kaiserman: "*WWD* uncompromisingly chooses what's best each season."

accentuate the line of a swimsuit; often she will experiment with different accessories to strengthen the total effect.

After the crew returns home, and the photographs are developed, the final phase—editing—begins. At this point the art director steps in to assist in the final selection. Hundreds of color slides laid out on light tables are carefully scrutinized by the art director and editor-in-chief. Those selected are made into prints, then incorporated in layouts that represent the magazine's fashion statement. If the art director and editor chose wisely and the photographer showed the clothes at their best, women across the country soon will be buying the creations of the designer featured.

Although most editors use their power judiciously, some have an inflated sense of their own importance. They concentrate almost exclusively on established designers because it takes more effort to explore the exciting and the offbeat and more courage to support them. Some editors accept or even demand free clothes from designers instead of buying the garments wholesale. Some aging editors refuse to relinquish prestigious positions whose demands they can no longer fulfill. Lazy editors specify studio sets instead of using actual locations; in the same way their subjects are often out of touch with reality. (How many women actually sit down to naïve little lunches with museum-quality place settings? How many own quaint vacation villas overlooking the Mediterranean Sea? How many can actually afford clothes like the Geoffrey Beene $1,890 green wool dress, loden tweed jacket, and red suede muffler suggested for a busy life-style?) Yet fashion magazines are in the business of propagating illusion at the same time that they fill the pocketbooks of couturiers, manufacturers, and retailers—and nourish but never quite satisfy the excessive appetites of style-hungry consumers. A smart editor is able to accommodate everyone.

Because fashion editors are always dashing to or from somewhere and perpetually racing to meet deadlines, it is amazing that they manage to retain their humor, sense of wonder, and unflagging enthusiasm year after year. Carrie Donovan, *The New York Times Magazine* fashion editor, is a case in point. Tuned in to the styles and trends to which her audience can relate, Donovan scours the market to select clothes that are functional rather than costumey. A typical story, such as "Saucy Spring Suits" (editors love alliteration), begins with a trip to the garment center a few short blocks from *The New York Times* office. As Donovan heads toward Calvin Klein's pristine, spacious showroom-workroom, she makes a mental note of an extravagant leather coat worn by a striking young woman walking past her on the street.

Toby Lerner (boutique buyer): "If you're in this business for any length of time, you realize it's a dance—with people changing partners from time to time."

Close friends, Donovan and Klein greet each other warmly. Klein invites Donovan and her free-lance stylist, who has just joined them, to preview slides of his men's line photographed on a spectacular model in atmospheric Boca Raton, Florida. A few minutes later one of Klein's assistants brings out a suit and matching crepe de chine blouse that Donovan considers "divine," the highest accolade that can be bestowed on a fashion, a fabric, or a designer. After she's selected other suits by other designers, the next step is to choose the accessories that will give them "a provocative new turn" and add excitement to the photographs. Some come from the designers; others—like a tippy hat, gold clover-shaped earrings, a brass-bead necklace, and high-heeled sandals—will be borrowed by the stylist.

After the clothes and accessories are ordered, Donovan and the stylist run through a list of models, looking for "someone who can carry this style." She rejects one candidate as "too boutiquey," then asks the stylist to determine whether one of her favorites will be available. While she's promising Klein an incredible photographer who is being "flown in from Paris for the shoot" (the fashion world tends to favor models and photographers from other parts of the world), one of the designer's assistants signs out the clothes, which will be returned after the sitting.

Next Donovan makes a quick visit to Donna Karan and Louis Dell'Olio of Anne Klein, whose showroom is in the same building. Another round of enthusiastic greetings ensues. Bolts of cloth are displayed, fabric swatches are pinned to the wall. Donovan spots a chic checked linen suit that is "just perfect," asks if there is a matching handbag, then flies out the door to another appointment.

On the day "Saucy Spring Suits" is shot, Donovan supervises every detail. When the photographs are processed, she selects the best images, works with her art director on the layout, writes lettuce-crisp copy, and checks captions. The result is a striking spread to which readers invariably respond.

Polly Allen Mellen, another respected fashion editor, has worked in the glamorous, chaotic world of publishing for the last twenty-four years. Ten years ago she left *Harper's Bazaar* for *Vogue,* where she is now fashion editor. A silver-haired, perennially young woman with sparkling eyes, an infectious smile, and marvelous tight, tanned skin, she exemplifies perfectly her belief that, "To look well is to feel well is to have a good time." Her taste is subtle; her look is always simple, tailored, and stylish.

One of those rare individuals who combine curiosity, wit, and brilliance, Mellen moves through fashion's labyrinthine maze with an unjaundiced eye and a consistent outpouring of original ideas. Her talent lies in an ability to be inspired month after month and invariably make a reader feel that a basic black cotton dress is essential on a summer day or that mixing designer clothes—a jacket from one with trousers from another—is a phenomenal idea. But she will not tout an unwearable fashion simply because it is new; rather Mellen attempts "to go a little further visually so that the reader (perhaps realizing that it's not quite her look) will find the clothes breathtaking—and at least nurture a new thought."

During a typical twelve-hour working day Mellen might help edit a designer's collection, suggesting that a skirt would look better in a brilliant purple or that a cropped jacket be tighter. As an incentive to create something spectacular in sequins, linen, cashmere, or terry cloth, she might inform designers that an upcoming *Vogue* editorial will feature blazers. In the office she edits copy, confers with the editorial board to select major themes for future issues ("Confetti Dots Are Sweeping the Country," "The Turquoise Story"), develops the "Vogue Woman of the Month" feature; chooses models and photographers, and supervises major shootings and all covers.

Asked to define the ideal *Vogue* cover girl, Polly Mellen specifies "open-faced, wide-eyed models (usually with honey-colored hair worn off the face) who range from eighteen to twenty-six. A girl's body is in better shape than a woman's, her skin is more resilient and can stand close-ups and the lens's penetration. The best cover girls have a piercing glance and a twinkle in their eyes. Unfortunately cover girls aren't born that often. There is no one to duplicate a Verushka or a Jean Shrimpton. We tend to use a few fabulous faces like Roseanne Vela, Patti Hansen, and Rene Russo repeatedly and occasionally celebrities who are beautiful and best sellers like Jackie Bisset, Cher, and Streisand."

It was the fashion press that made these entertainers into fashion celebrities and that made the careers of many successful models, photographers, and designers. And it is the fashion editor whose approval makes all the difference in the fashion world.

THE BUYER

THE BOTTOM LINE

Suddenly designers are showing necklines slit to the navel, knee-grazing hems, tight skirts, see-through tops. The new look, an antidote to the now-passé layered effect, is fresh and fabulous on elegantly proportioned runway models. But is it suitable for the average customer? Will it sell? Only the buyer, who orders the merchandise that stocks the stores, can toss that proverbial bouquet of approval by spending her employer's money on body-revealing styles with shorter hemlines.

Because women have always had a greater interest than men in acquiring a new wardrobe rather than simply replacing old clothes, it is not surprising that they dominate the retailing profession. There are thousands of buyers, representing large and small stores that they own or for which they work, but only the exceptional ones have that rapid-fire talent for making important decisions quickly, choosing the right styles in the right combinations and price range to suit a specific clientele, and giving that clientele enough good reasons to restock their closets each season.

To do her job well, a buyer must be intimately involved with the moods and motives of her customers; she may adore Armani, but she nevertheless realizes that her clients in Albuquerque may not share her preference. Whether she is checking out a new resource or one that's old and trusted, she is always conscious of the consumer. A buyer for Fiorucci, a young, exciting shop specializing in disco gear and whimsical clothes, chooses merchandise far different from that ordered by a Saks Fifth Avenue contemporary sportswear buyer, who seeks well-made garments that won't overpower the wearer. And an experienced buyer is aware of whether her customers are responsive to new fashions or whether they lag behind a season or two before adopting them, whether they buy mainly for status or for practicality.

Carla Araque shows a flowing Halston evening gown for representatives from department stores and boutiques across the country.

A buyer must possess an instinctive creative flair for spotting emerging trends and determining which will work for her clientele; because it takes months to produce and ship merchandise from different parts of the world, she takes a calculated risk by anticipating in January what customers will buy in August. Because her customers spend fortunes on evening clothes, a buyer from a specialty shop in Texas makes a point of attending the same charity balls and observing their tastes. Another buyer spends part of each day on the retail floor of her department to determine why certain clothes are rejected. Still another, despite her conviction that disco music was destroying her inner ear, went to the hottest club in town to see firsthand what the sartorial pacesetters were wearing.

Aside from her scrutiny of the fashion world a buyer must be alert to developments in the textile industry and keep abreast of what's available where in the world market; in Milan, for example, she finds fine tailoring, while New York is best for casual wear, California for active sports clothes. Paris provides elegance and the unexpected, and London is a prime source for knits.

Aside from withstanding the physical and emotional pressures of frequent international buying trips and visits to designers' showrooms, the buyer is also responsible for running her department. Concerned with the day-to-day details of business management, she always knows how much stock must be bought and how much can be expected to be sold. Among the frustrations she frequently endures are shortages of a popular item or an overstock of something that is selling poorly; overstocking, moreover, may deplete her budget and deprive her of the opportunity to pick up on new trends.

When the merchandise she's ordered arrives at the store, it must be sorted, counted, price marked, pressed, and checked for workmanship, style, and size. Acting as administrator, psychologist, diplomat, and idea person, the buyer oversees these procedures. She also explains the selling points of new merchandise to the sales force, sometimes even requesting that they wear the clothes while working. She keeps records of inventory and sales on a daily, weekly, monthly, and yearly basis (large stores employ computers to determine what has been sold and what is in stock). She responds to customers' complaints and requests for special orders and appears on the sales floor at its busiest periods. And, in between her periodic buying trips, she sets time aside to appraise the work of new designers.

Buyers who work in large establishments compete intramurally as well as with other stores for the customer's dollar. To lure shoppers into her own department, she must convince the store's fashion director to display her offerings in the most prominent windows and ensure that she has enough stock to back up the presentation. She must convey the excitement she feels about the new garments to the personnel in her department as well as to the copywriter responsible for the store's advertising. To attract the attention of customers within the store, she will install provocative items at the entrance to the department and create a stimulating environment within; junior clothes may be shown in a simulated discotheque complete with nonstop music. To dress up the sales floor, she may borrow objects like an antique organ or Balinese puppets from other parts of the store. Mannequins must be imaginatively accessorized and the merchandise carefully placed for easy viewing and access. Common devices to promote sales in individual departments include designer and celebrity appearances; luncheons featuring a fashion editor or designer; videotaped fashion shows and interviews with designers; "dressing for success" workshops; informal fashion shows in which models parade around the store displaying a card with the designer's name; blown-up photographs of celebrities wearing a particular fashion item; and a new designer's clothes obtained on an exclusive basis. Some buyers, like Henri Bendel's Marion Greenberg, will accommodate customers by pulling together a complete look with accessories gathered from other departments.

Each and every working day a buyer concentrates on topping previous sales figures as well as coping with the internal pressures created by working for the benefit of a specific department rather than the good of the store. Her struggle for more floor space, more advertising, and more frequent window display is constant. Buyers in one major New York department store are so intensely competitive that they pass each other daily without acknowledgment. If one of them discovers a wonderful new manufacturer (or, in buyers' lingo, a resource) that is too expensive for her department, she may intentionally forget to convey the information to the appropriate colleague. A buyer might select a designer's line for the junior department, even though the clothes would sell better in another part of the store. She might even steal the scarce mannequin supports called T-stands from other departments after the store closes for the day.

But these inordinate pressures diminish when a buyer discovers a new talent. Eagle-eyed Mildred Custin, former president of the now defunct Bonwit Teller, believed in Calvin Klein and was first to order his coats; his success enhanced her own reputation. Moreover a successful buyer can earn up to $50,000 per year along with stock options and other perquisites. And if she's very good at her job, she has the thrill of knowing that her decision resulted in millions of dollars of profits for the store.

Before undertaking a market trip that could result in those profits, a buyer refers to a number of reliable sources that telegraph upcoming fashion messages. Trade publications such as *Women's Wear Daily, Daily News Record, The Ram Report,* and *California Apparel Report* are invaluable; so are European fashion magazines that show clothes that don't hit America until six months later. Subscriptions to fashion services like *Nigel French Enterprises, Here & There, Toby,* and *IM* cost thousands of dollars each, but provide up-to-the-minute accounts of new trends in the form of comprehensive reports, audio-visual materials that recap the collections, color charts, and fabric boards. The weekly *Fashion Calendar,* an invaluable subscription-only guide, lists fashion shows here and abroad, showroom openings of seasonal lines, and special fashion events such as the Whitney Museum's twenty-five-year retrospective of Missoni clothes and fabrics and the spectacular Diaghilev show organized by Diana Vreeland at the Metropolitan Museum of Art.

Not all buyers see everything offered by even the most popular designers. For one thing it's impossible; there are thousands of apparel companies in Manhattan alone. That's why store and individual buyers throughout the country rely on resident buying offices in resource-stocked cities to do their reconnaissance work. Acting as the eyes, ears, and legs of its affiliates, a resident buying office supplies a buyer with relevant market information and, upon request, makes purchases. Independent or store owned, these offices are similar to the stores that they service with one major exception: they don't sell merchandise. Resident buying offices employ their own buyers to review collections, then send out special distribution letters in support of specific items (their recommendations are generally followed by store buyers, who know that resident buyers put their reputations on the line with such endorsements). In addition the resident offices mail out reports on market activities; hold preview clinics of upcoming trends; suggest ideas for publicity, display, catalogs, and fashion shows; prod manufacturers to deliver merchandise on time, especially for buyers who can't visit Manhattan frequently; conduct group-buying programs to achieve reduced prices and better delivery; maintain foreign offices to facilitate foreign purchases; search out exclusive items; and take designer merchandise to the Far East to have it "knocked off"—duplicated at a lower price.

The most influential resident buying office in terms of sales volume, size, and the prestige of its affiliates is Associated Merchandising Corpo-

Buyers are presented with all of the glitter the industry can muster—
here Tharita models a Bill Kaiserman creation.

ration (AMC). For its buying and counseling services AMC receives a percentage of the sales from forty-seven noncompetitive members in the States and abroad. AMC's exuberant vice-president and merchandise manager, Bernie Ozer, is one of the fashion industry's most striking figures (when he visits Japan, he is often mistaken for Sydney Greenstreet) as well as one of the most competent. Twenty-five years of experience, a capable staff, and a highly professional eye enable him to discover the best in fashion from junior sportswear to intimate apparel. As Jean Wallrapp of Glenora told *WWD*, "You're trying to show Ozer the collection, and he's conducting a wild show. You yell, 'Bernie, pay attention!' He looks up, points to the rack, and says, 'I like that, change that, that has to go,' and he's right. He doesn't miss a beat."

On his daily walks along Broadway and Seventh Avenue, Ozer, the peripatetic David Merrick of the garment center, exchanges the latest news, gossip, and highs and lows of the market with manufacturers and designers who want him to evaluate their lines. When he gets wind of a hot trend, he flashes the news to members of AMC via phone, Telex, personal meetings, weekly bulletins, fashion shows, major reports before "market week," and slide presentations; they in turn place orders that can attract customers who want the latest merchandise.

Although Ozer's trips to Europe, India, and the Orient have yielded a number of hot items, he defines his job as "influencing the total mixture of merchandise in a store, innovating and expanding new fashion ideas, and encouraging new talent." Aided in no small part by his flexibility, willingness to make mistakes, and unerring originality, Ozer is one of the few who has mastered fashion's silken jungle and provoked some of its more enduring legends. As designer Betsey Johnson notes, "Ozer has a sense of humor and knows what designers are about—and AMC is hot and hip."

But reports from a resident buying office and from the fashion press are not enough to prepare a buyer for a buying trip. Her instincts and her research must be supplemented by meetings with her store's fashion director. It is the latter who produces and sustains a coordinated fashion image—trendy, chic, or traditional—for the entire store; without her unifying overview, each department would reflect only its buyer's personal ideas. Unknown outside the industry, the fashion director—with support from top management—plans promotions, revamps shops, and oversees windows, interior display, and catalogs. Aware of the workings of each department under her supervision, she advises buyers on what is best for their customers and makes sure that accessories are available to coordinate with the coats, suits, and dresses that are being promoted.

To predict what styles are forthcoming, a fashion director visits Europe and New York; using slides, sketches, and swatches, she will inform that store's staff of events in the shrinking fashion universe before they actually place their orders. Occasionally a fashion director suggests purchasing a line that a buyer detests; fearful of refusing, the rebellious buyer might retaliate by choosing the worst styles and least attractive colors and fabrics. She risks losing money for her department, but she will never be asked to buy from that manufacturer again.

Among the outstanding fashion directors at work today are Ellin Saltzman of Saks Fifth Avenue, Anita Gallo of B. Altman, Terry Melville of Macy's, Dawn Mello of Bergdorf Goodman, Geraldine Stutz (the only female and longest-tenured president of a major fashion department store) of Henri Bendel, and Kal Ruttenstein of Bloomingdale's.

Bloomingdale's is definitely the store that everyone wants to see—even if it is only to browse for new ideas. Merchandise from all over the world is stocked to supply an upwardly mobile society with every imaginable product—and then some. Retailers from as far away as Tokyo photograph the ingenious window displays for possible adaptation at home, and it is the one store that Queen Elizabeth requested to see on her trip to America. Fortunately Ruttenstein, the only man in this distinguished group, never seems to run out of ideas. Refusing to rest on Bloomingdale's laurels, he generates continuous excitement by setting up mini-shops that exist for four to six weeks and feature everything from aprons to underwear, and he maintains a show-biz atmosphere with frequent designer appearances and store-wide promotions.

Ruttenstein, the energetic staff of fashion coordinators who assist him, and his buyers are constantly on the lookout for new resources. His trips to Paris are always productive; when he saw a bustier (a strapless form-fitting top), he sensed the impact it would have; soon American manufacturers were producing the item for Bloomingdale's fourteen stores. After one of his fashion coordinators showed Ruttenstein a huge array of fanciful polka-dotted fabrics gathered at Interstoff, the trendy textile fair held annually in Frankfurt, Germany, he enlivened January, "the toughest month of the year," by turning an entire floor of the store into a polka-dotted paradise. Although most customers had little money left after Christmas-buying binges, thousands were nonetheless seized with an overwhelming urge to fortify their dull winter wardrobes when they were bombarded with polka-dotted Bloomingdale's ads and saw floors, walls, accessories, clothes, and windows covered with dots in every conceivable color and size.

Terry Melville, Macy's irreverent fashion director for juniors, has a supersensitive built-in radar system that enables her to clock the latest trends and get them to her mercurial young customers in record time. Although Macy's boasts two million square feet of selling space, one need never leave Melville's domain to get a bite to eat or buy a fabulous poster, a pair of slim suede trousers, a rainbow-hued leotard, glittery face powder, a bowling shirt, or even vitamins. To fulfill her concepts, an inexhaustible staff of display people transforms the fourth floor into an ever-changing arcade of mini-shops, a concept pioneered twenty years ago by Bendel's Gerri Stutz. Recent boutiques—on the order of Shape-Up, Locker Room, Roller Disco, Poster and Picture Disco, Self-Center for health products, and Dressing with Flavor to purvey fruit-printed clothes and fruit-scented shampoos—have anticipated the tastes of her clientele. To create an incomparable disco look perfect for her trendy customers, Melville once augmented a plain gray sweat shirt and sweat pants with unique accessories: extravagant ankle-strapped sandals, an embroidered silk kimono, a purple boa, and a tiny Oriental brocade evening bag.

While fashion directors are at work maintaining the store's persona, the buyers place orders to keep up with manufacturers' new offerings throughout the year. The most frenetic buying takes place during semiannual market weeks (actually ten-day periods) that begin in Europe with a comprehensive education in the most advanced looks. Depending on their specialties, buyers visit Florence, Milan, Paris, or London in April for the fall-winter collections and again in October for spring-summer. In Paris some twenty-five thousand foreign buyers are welcome at a twelve-hundred-booth trade show featuring clothes from all over the world, and they are happily received in showrooms—as long as they bring a checkbook. Before they admit buyers, some designers demand a minimum commitment; Kenzo, for instance, requires $16,000.

The shows are spectacular; so are the effects. In the spring of 1979, some forty Paris houses willingly spent thousands of dollars to show their latest ready-to-wear collections (perhaps because the French women's clothing industry made $702 million in exports the year before). For the first time most designers held shows in the same place: four enormous tents erected at Les Halles. As usual everyone clambered for front-row seats; some buyers even switched the place cards taped to the chairs. Top European and American models (predominantly long-legged black beau-

ties) strode down the runway to the sound of American jazz tunes. Some
wore clothes that the designers knew would never go into production—
there simply aren't enough clients willing to purchase outrageous creations. But the more extravagant looks generate headlines along with interest in more saleable items like designer-labeled scarves, jewelry,
lingerie, and perfume. Each designer shows something memorable, a life-
time of culture and style expressed in each season's collection. Certain
designers hold particular attraction for buyers; everyone goes to Paris to
see what the avant-garde—Thierry Mugler, Claude Montana, Yves St.
Laurent, and Kenzo—are up to.

Unlike the press, buyers do not have the clout to guarantee instanta-
neous fame to a designer. Regarded in the European market as mere
clothing merchants, they may be relegated to the balconies of enormous
halls, where twenty-five hundred tickets are distributed for two thousand
seats, or they are forced to crash shows along with several thousand fero-
cious fashion mavens by shouting the magic word, "Press!" But no matter

how badly buyers may be treated, they shop Europe because of its advanced attitude toward shape and fabric. Even if a scant percentage of American shoppers relate to a radical silhouette, its inclusion creates an air of excitement in a department or shop. Experimental fashion attracts a forward-looking young professional who is beginning to regard clothing as an investment—an attitude long prevalent in Europe. Older, more traditional customers, meanwhile, buy from familiar designers whose clothes vary infinitesimally from season to season.

Forgoing lunch at one of Paris's famous restaurants, a buyer may browse through some of the city's six thousand boutiques in search of something new and spectacular that hasn't already been copied by an American manufacturer. If she represents a large store, she may arrange to have her finds duplicated in bulk; a buyer from a small store or boutique may simply buy as many pieces as she can. Despite her personal preferences, an expert buyer always remembers that she is in business to please her customers; if they are conservative, she'll buy that lacy garter belt or those silk stockings for herself.

Walking briskly through Paris, she searches for an outrageous fashion item to exhibit; she knows that French women collectively zero in on one fabulous idea at a time, making new trends readily identifiable. She observes the anonymous young people with their Mickey Mouse watches, innumerable silk scarves in muted tones wrapping their throats, hand-knit leg warmers, glittering anklets and Mao sandals; perhaps she'll snap a picture of a woman in a World War II leather paratrooper's helmet. Last spring American apparel people noted that French women were wearing expensive, skintight leather jeans, classic silk blouses, long pearl ropes, and unconstructed skirts; no doubt American women will be moving in that direction this year.

In the afternoon the buyers and their fashion director (if they represent a large store) will attend still more fashion shows. If the clothes are something that they know their customers can't live without, they will take voluminous notes; if not, they fill only one or two pages of their ever-present notebooks. At night there is little energy remaining for Paris's hottest disco. Instead each buyer tries to digest all that she's seen, edits the best for her clientele, soaks her feet, and prepares for another mind-boggling, exhausting day of yet more fashion shows.

Although the Paris collections are noted for their explosive experimentalism, buyers who complain about French rudeness and the impossibly high cost of room and board are increasingly visiting Milan as well. Italy has always offered finely woven fabrics, but over the last six years

Bernie Ozer, the David Merrick of the fashion world,
strolling along his beloved Seventh Avenue.

certain ready-to-wear designers have become phenomenally successful. Among this group, all of whom make high-styled, highly appreciated, and very expensive contemporary classics, are Mila Schon, Gianni Versace, the Fendis (the most exclusive furriers in the world), Basile, and Krizia. At one point Versace's clothes were so coveted by New York buyers that he found himself in the enviable position of deciding which stores would get which styles on an exclusive basis.

There is barely time for the buyer to digest what she's seen in the European collections, in the boutiques, and on the streets before she's back in New York for another round of fashion shows punctuated by a steady disco beat or a rhythmic samba. Lights flash, skaters poised like wild birds skim by, and confetti falls over the jet-lagged audience as they view still more clothes.

Buyers from large stores visit the New York market six to eight times per year. Designer clothes for fall can be seen in April and May. In September holiday wear is offered; from September 15 through October it's resort and cruisewear. From October 15 through November buyers shop for spring fashions; in January, for summer; and in May for transitional clothes. Some twenty-five thousand independent buyers also visit New York several times annually to fill their boutiques with clothes to which their customers can relate.

Arriving in New York on the Sunday evening before market week begins, a typical buyer checks into a conveniently located hotel. On Monday morning she meets with the independent buyer from her resident buying office to discuss trends and review the best of what the market has to offer. If her schedule is too demanding, she may see only those glittering fashion shows held in the evening and usually preceded by cocktail parties. She will set up appointments with manufacturers (who keep their showrooms open at night and on weekends to accommodate buyers) in order of their importance. Naturally she favors resources who promise prompt delivery of clothes in the right colors, sizes, fabrics, styles, and prices. She may visit 512 Seventh Avenue for young designer sportswear but avoid 550 Seventh Avenue if her budget is not large enough for her to place a minimum order with certain top designers in residence there; in that case she will try to find that marvelous Joan Crawford jacket and those pleated trousers elsewhere. Sometimes she will be disappointed in her efforts; if *WWD* features a particular designer on its cover and his company is besieged with buyers, he tends to give preference to those with larger budgets. During "free" moments she darts in and out of stores checking labels, follows up new resources, scrutinizes street fashion, and tries to see at least one Broadway hit.

Maggie Han for Krizia, awaiting her turn on the runway before hundreds of guests.

A typical working day for the buyer visiting New York begins after breakfast and continues nonstop through late afternoon. During each showroom visit she takes notes for future reference; otherwise each line merges into the others until they form a hopeless blur in her mind. Seated at a small table, she listens to the hyperbolic speeches of a salesperson who displays the new clothes and talks up their best features. If the buyer feels certain about a particular suede suit or charmeuse separates, she writes an order immediately. If not, she waits until she gets home to regain a clear-eyed perspective. After trying to second-guess her customers by carefully editing all that she has seen, a buyer will order the best and most diversified merchandise for her department—and hope it arrives on time.

All buyers are treated courteously; some buyers from major specialty stores, like I. Magnin with its twenty-three branches, are treated even more courteously. When Maureen Wool, an attractive, platinum-haired sportswear buyer for I. Magnin's San Francisco branch, visits a showroom, she receives the red-carpet treatment—it is no secret that her visit can mean an order of at least $25,000. As a salesperson displays his offerings, he asks Wool's opinion of the shaped silhouette, brighter colors, and competitors' lines. Wool pores over color swatch books, chooses a variety of printed and solid silk separates, ignores the more conservatively styled linens, discusses the method and dates of delivery, and places her order immediately; the merchandise manager, her direct superior, will confirm it later on. If Wool feels that a line has potential but isn't quite right for her style-conscious customers, she might collaborate with the manufacturer on restyling before writing an order.

Whether clothes are bought in Europe or America, a strong rapport between designer and buyer benefits both. Once they've established a good working relationship, the buyer will get preferred deliveries and, sometimes, huge photographic blowups of the merchandise for display purposes. She will be allowed to return styles that haven't sold, and a designer or his representative may visit her store with a trunk show featuring the newest designs. A designer or manufacturer with an engaging personality can motivate a buyer to order or reorder. If two firms are equal in price and quality, she will gravitate toward the company from whom she gets that extra bit of attention.

Because buyers and manufacturers need one another to prosper, one would assume that their relationship would be smooth. It isn't always; unadulterated self-interest on either side has contributed to fashion's reputation as a cutthroat business. By promising a full-page ad and window coverage, for example, a buyer may obtain exclusive rights to a line, then renege on the order at the last minute. She may phone in an order but never confirm it with the requisite signature from the merchandise manager or, even worse, deny the order was ever placed at all because she later learned that her department was overstocked. A buyer who inherits a poorly managed department may try to alter, decrease, or cancel orders. A buyer from a powerful store can choose to mark down clothes that aren't moving and make the manufacturer absorb the loss; a blouse that wholesales for $15 and sells at $30 may be reduced to $20, in which case the manufacturer is paid $10 instead of the $15 previously agreed upon. A manufacturer who refuses to take the loss will be summarily dropped as a future resource.

Buyers know their power, and those with overinflated egos grossly abuse it. Some are infamous for returning merchandise without the manufacturer's permission; canceling appointments at the last minute; recklessly ordering more than necessary and then canceling if goods don't arrive on time; or purchasing more than the monthly budget allows and then penalizing the manufacturer by sending back the clothes.

But manufacturers aren't always victims. The flattery showered on an important buyer may border on the absurd; "You look fabulous! Darling, you've lost so much weight!" and "You look ten years younger" are standard Seventh Avenue greetings and represent affection that lasts as long as the buyer deals with the firm. Moreover a manufacturer may promise an exclusive to a jubilant buyer, who later discovers that the so-called exclusive was given to her nearest competitor as well. A manufacturer may immediately fulfill a large order and then ship smaller orders to less important buyers at a much later date, necessitating huge markdowns because at the end of the season the clothes are no longer appropriate. Or he may make beautifully constructed samples but ship ill-fitting clothes in the wrong colors, styles, or sizes. He may even drop a line that didn't receive enough general interest without informing those buyers who had placed orders for it.

There are those buyers who can't endure the daily frustrations of dealing with firms that promise one thing and deliver another. They resent the hardships of meeting and beating last year's figures and spending years as an assistant because top-echelon buyers rarely quit. They are frequently exhausted from extensive traveling. That's why many become creative assistants to the manufacturer who welcomed their suggestions to taper a sleeve, widen a lapel, or narrow a skirt. Others use experience gained from running a department in a large store to establish their own boutiques, where they no longer have to answer to merchandise managers, fashion directors, vice-presidents, and presidents.

For those who remain in their jobs, particularly the good ones, no two days are alike. Gambling thousands of dollars on an upcoming trend and retaining a sense of humor as pressures mount (and they always do), the best buyer refuses to play it safe—if she did, she wouldn't be in fashion.

STORE WINDOWS

DREAMS ON SALE

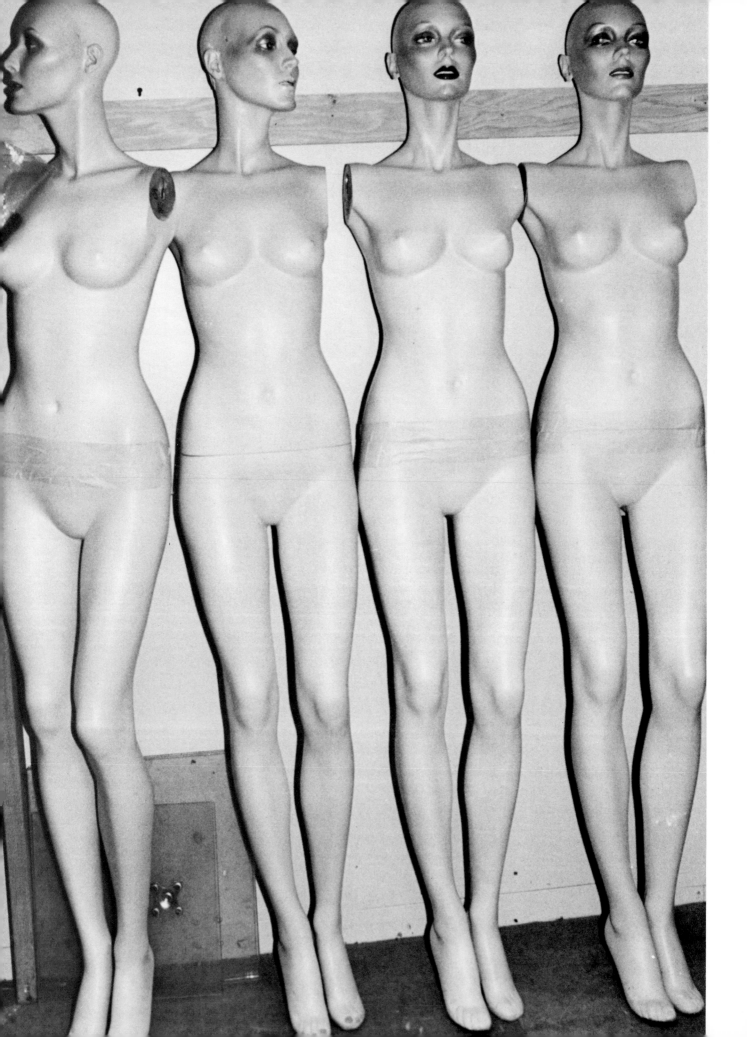

Today's store window is a showcase for the talents of a display designer as well as for the merchandise within. Window dressers have created a new art form in three dazzling dimensions that puts the magic back into fashion merchandising. In *Windows,* a photography book devoted to this irreverent genre, Michael Emory described "a small but noisy revolution . . . its main battleground is midtown Manhattan, but shock waves have been felt throughout the country, from the smallest boutiques to the most prestigious department stores. A dynamic new approach has been initiated by designers determined to shock, amuse, or seduce buyers into a new awareness of display."

Before display achieved its newfound cachet, windows rarely captured the attention of passersby. There was no drama, no theater. Because designers lacked freedom or imagination or both, the only discernible themes were holidays or the changing seasons. When windows did tell a story, it was inevitably a weak one. Clothes never quite fit the static mannequins meant to show them off; the most splendid garments hung listlessly on dressmaker forms or were stacked haphazardly on the floor. Customers were enticed more frequently by "sale" signs than by the displays.

In the past originality was occasionally in evidence—but only occasionally. Surrealist artist Salvador Dali once plunged through Bonwit Teller's Fifth Avenue window, and in the 1960s up-and-coming artists Jasper Johns and Robert Rauschenberg designed windows for the same store. But it wasn't until the 1970s that clever store owners began to realize that provocative windows could lure shoppers inside. Now windows have become full-fledged attractions for both tourists and art lovers. In New York City, the mecca of display, certain store windows are more vital and aesthetically pleasing than work shown by some fine artists in antiseptic galleries; display designers from other parts of the world make it a point to study and sometimes photograph those that are most memora-

Along with the irreverence and subtle sense of irony that characterize a successful window, the new lifelike mannequins have made window display one of merchandising's most effective tools. A relatively recent phenomenon, these stunning "creatures" are manufactured by a half-dozen major supply houses or their scores of imitators located in New York City. Just as clothing buyers descend on the city during market week, window dressers flock to the display houses in June and December when new models are introduced. When they order mannequins, they specify skin tone, wig color, and whether or not to apply permanent makeup.

Most display designers consider Adel Rootstein's U.S.A., Inc. the best and most innovative of the suppliers. For the last ten years, Rootstein has satisfied an international clientele—including most of the prestigious Fifth Avenue stores—with stock from her "wax museum" in New York's SoHo or its counterparts in London, Stockholm, and Paris. Her customized mannequins, which are designed in London and cost about $500, are available in a wide range of contemporary types from superchic to rainbow-haired punk rocker.

Rootstein makes it a habit to scout for new faces. Her mannequins include doubles of top models like Toukie Smith, who became Bloomingdale's first black mannequin, and Pat Cleveland. If their look appeals to her, Rootstein will even ask striking-looking strangers on the street or guests at a party to join her famed collection. When she saw model Sara Kapp on the pages of *Vogue,* Rootstein took her to lunch and invited her to England for a month of almost daily posing. Like all Rootstein's mannequins, Kapp's likeness was modeled in clay, then cast as a six-foot-tall, twenty-five-pound, size-ten plaster dummy available in a range of postures and with any number of facial expressions. As a result, the cool, sloe-eyed Kapp is admired by window-shoppers on streets as far away as Tokyo.

But even the best mannequins are not enough to ensure an effective display; they must be used advantageously. Those windows that seem most effortless often involve the most time, energy, and expense. Each window is designed to maximize existing space. Painted or fabric-covered panels in dark colors or neutral tones suggest an endless horizon; a small area appears less constricted when mannequins are placed in a seated position; and a single mannequin used without props opens up the space still more.

Merchandise must also be appropriately scaled to the window's size.

One of Bob Currie's window displays at Bendel's in New York.

Tiffany's Gene Moore, who has never repeated a single design during his long career, uses perspective, scale, lighting, and color so skillfully that the entranced viewer totally forgets that these windows are Fifth Avenue's smallest.

Just as lighting creates startling effects on a theatrical stage, it can work equal wonders in a window. A display director hires skilled electricians to create an atmosphere that complements the clothes being shown; blue light generally flatters daytime garments, whereas pink light adds a romantic glow to evening fashions. Special templates attached to projectors can simulate shooting stars, a snowfall, a hot sun, and other special effects, while pinpoint lighting (or spotlights) emphasizes a jewel, the cut of a shoe, or a stylish sleeve. Color is equally important; a designer familiar with its psychological effects uses the appropriate shade to produce a desired mood—green for relaxation, red for excitement, blue for serenity, yellow for gaiety.

Unless the display director intends to divert attention from the clothes, he chooses props that enhance rather than detract from them. To accentuate the kaleidoscopic turquoise, red, fuchsia, and purple colors of Stephen Burrows's designs, Saks Fifth Avenue's Bob Benzio used an olive drab background and a motorized mobile suspended from the ceiling. Tiffany's Gene Moore frequently employs commonplace objects—scales, telephone wire, thick-plaited rope, ice picks, paint cans and brushes—as a perfect counterpoint to the exquisite jewels that are the point of his displays.

Although the fashion office decides what merchandise to feature in which windows—to encourage a quick sale or to show off the store's timeliness—a creative window dresser can make his feelings known. By subtly manipulating the window's physical environment, he can downgrade clothes that he personally dislikes. For example, unappealing garments are easily overwhelmed by magnificent props (Art Deco furniture, Greek sculpture, richly embroidered Indian cushions); by extravagant coiffures (a Gibson Girl look, sleek hair falling to a mannequin's waist); or by unusual accessories (armloads of gigantic ivory bracelets, a garland of silk flowers worn as a necklace). Mannequins are sometimes positioned with their backs to the street, concealed behind ornate screens that reveal only a small piece of a garment, or grouped with other mannequins to minimize details of the clothes.

Although Henri Bendel has only two large windows, its free-lance display director, Bob Currie, ensures that their impact is stunning. When he was asked to show dresses with tie-dyed markings that resembled birch

bark, he camouflaged them behind a forest of birch trees, and even their
designer was unaware that Currie wasn't wild about the look. At other
times Currie has devoted one of the windows of the luxurious specialty
shop to a single fantastic mannequin in juxtaposition to four less exciting
figures in the other.

Even when one fashion designer's work is featured in the windows of
two stores, the clothes look entirely different because they must reflect
each store's individual image. Saks Fifth Avenue evokes old money and a
family orientation, for example, while Fiorucci is young and outrageous.
Bendel's treats fashion with a sense of humor and is noted for advanced
styling in small sizes. Bloomingdale's, a cultural phenomenon, generates
excitement about everything it promotes, and it promotes everything
from chocolate-chip cookies to lizard belts to the state of Israel. B. Alt-

man is a calm, tasteful, traditional store; Lord & Taylor offers the best American design; genteel Bergdorf Goodman caters to wealthy customers who love European designers and haute couture; and Macy's, the world's largest department store, is famous for constantly renovating, refurbishing, and upgrading its image.

Within the context of a store's personality a creative display designer can reveal his own anxieties and fantasies. Some base windows on topical situations. A New York newspaper strike prompted Bonwit Teller's Richard Cartledge to decorate the windows with enormous letters spelling out the names of various papers; elegantly dressed mannequins were visible in the background. The Richard Avedon retrospective at the Metropolitan Museum of Art motivated Candy Pratts of Bloomingdale's to cover an entire wall of a Lexington Avenue window with Avedon's magnificent black-and-white photographs.

Although a look behind the scenes at a department store strips away illusions of glamour and dispels the inevitable aura of mystery, it reveals a beehive of activity that is just as exciting as a finished window display. A visit to Bergdorf Goodman's display department, which has an annual budget of about $2 million, is a case in point.

To prepare for the new window displays on view each Thursday, work begins the day before. A few minutes after 6:00 P.M. on any Wednesday evening, the only sounds on Bergdorf's main floor come from workmen hammering, painting, and building "rooms." Light-footed window trimmers are transporting last week's mannequins by express elevator to the display department (constant handling necessitates their refurbishing every six months); others are carefully hanging clothes on racks or returning accessories to the right departments.

Bergdorf's owns some three hundred mannequins. The large display room is a hodgepodge of heads attached to torsos, scattered limbs, and fully assembled dummies leaning against the walls. Variously colored wigs and boxes of jewelry, scarves, hose, and shoes are strewn about. A cosmetic case overflows with every conceivable shade of lipstick, rouge, eye shadow, liner, and pencil. In the middle of the room stands Larry Laslo, Bergdorf's exuberant display director, who is also responsible for interior boutiques and displays. Now he is *issuing* directives to a staff of twenty-five, fifteen of whom are free-lance trimmers who work for $3.50 per hour. Only one of the assistants is female; the necessity of dragging heavy mannequins across the floor has discouraged many women from entering the field.

For Laslo inspiration for a window comes from seeing a designer's work either on the runway or at the showroom. As a result of a recent visit with John Anthony, Laslo has decided to place the designer's classical clothes against iridescent brown silk panels; antique sculpture on pedestals will accentuate their timeless appeal. Assistants are dressing several mannequins whose posture best displays these particular clothes; a slit skirt is emphasized on a figure whose legs are extended. The dummies' hands and arms are removed to facilitate dressing. Gloves are slit down the back for easy fit, and boots must be forced onto their feet.

An elegant, pin-striped buyer from the couture department stops by to put his stamp of approval on the accessories selected from the store's stock to complement these clothes. Behind him the mannequins are being covered with smocks to prevent damaging their garments while they're made up. Last week's makeup is removed with alcohol or Fantastik. Then Laslo or an assistant will spend up to an hour painting each beautiful porcelain-based face with watercolors and a variety of cosmetics. Aware of Anthony's preference for subdued tones, Laslo watches closely to make sure that colors are subtle. Powdered cheekbones are accentuated with brown shadow, then rouged with terra-cotta; lips are outlined and filled in with a burnished peach tone under a light gloss. The bottoms of the eyes are accentuated with purple to add depth before lids are shadowed in a subtle lavender. For variety blue eyes are sometimes painted over brown ones. Kneecaps are rouged, cleavages powdered, and fingernails painted.

Laslo holds a strawberry-blond wig next to a wine velvet suit to see whether the colors will work together. He then instructs an assistant to style a chestnut-colored wig into a dramatic rolled hairdo inspired by a striking photo in Italian *Bazaar* (photographers and display directors admit that they feed off one another in their endless effort to present fashion more provocatively). Hair is pinned back with carpet tacks and lightly sprayed before a tiny, frivolous hat is nailed in place.

Magically transformed by the display team, the mannequins have gradually assumed characters of their own: vibrant, tantalizing, elusive, flirtatious. Now they are transported by elevator to the main floor, where the newly prepared windows are awaiting them. The clothes they are wearing determine which of the seventeen Bergdorf's windows they will occupy; displays on Fifty-seventh Street tend to be humorous or even campy, whereas those on Fifth Avenue are more conservative and showcase established designers. As each of this crop is wired in the appropriate place to avoid slippage, Laslo spots a flaw in one of the brown silk panels. Rather than complain to an assistant, he climbs a twenty-foot ladder and restaples the fabric himself.

Bergdorf Goodman's windows.

It is time to design the lighting, which is dictated by Laslo's desire to emphasize a shoe, a jewel, or a cascading skirt. He specifies an amber gel to give one window a warm glow, then dashes outside to assess the effect. Each time the lights are adjusted—warmed or cooled or heightened or dimmed—Laslo returns to the street. The process will be repeated perhaps fifteen times before he dismisses his staff and heads home, bleary-eyed but exhilarated at having seen his ideas become reality. And all week long, passersby marveling at the exquisite windows will be oblivious to the nail supporting a mannequin's heel, the pins holding a skirt in place, or the cans of spray paint stored just beyond the valances.

Laslo's signature is a pared-down yet opulent look featuring a work of art in one form or another; Oriental antiques, French furniture, Moroccan rugs, a jungle of bamboo, or fresh flowers accentuate precisely composed windows that make little social or political comment.

Venezuelan-born free-lance designer Victor Hugo, on the other hand, creates windows for Halston's Madison Avenue shop that combine social analysis with a healthy helping of black humor. He is fortunate in that Halston allows him to present merchandise in an amusing, sophisticated way, and he is clever enough to produce displays in only one window that are sometimes spectacular and often irresistible. Hugo regards his windows as a continuing soap opera. Capitalizing on real-life situations, he bases his "weekly paintings" on subjects such as the bombing at LaGuardia Airport, Patty Hearst's trial (portrayed in three "chapters"), and a woman giving birth in a hospital room. Because he feels that the viewer's reactions complete his work, Hugo plays with them and encourages them to interpret the scenes.

To heighten a dramatic situation, he occasionally alters his window midweek. To finish the pregnancy scene, for instance, he placed a baby in the woman's arms. One viewer responded to this alteration by scrawling across the glass, "This is very sick." To end the airport scene, the energetic Hugo destroyed it at 5:00 one morning—as if there had been an actual bombing. Observing that the mannequins and clothes had been torn apart, an unsuspecting woman, imagining that a bomb had been set off in the window, called the police.

Equally provocative was Hugo's "rape" window, in which a beautifully dressed woman (in a Halston, of course) was portrayed lying on her back outside a theater. Her handbag was open, money displayed. With these clues the public was left to interpret the scenario for themselves—and they did. The usually blasé Madison Avenue strollers could not pass by without some very pointed comments.

Because the silver and white mannequins that Halston bought when he opened the shop are ageless and faceless, Hugo feels that the viewer can project herself into the scenes in his windows. "It would be awful if I had to use mannequins with faces," Hugo notes, "because they either look like prostitutes off Forty-second Street or bland models." Bored with the displays he sees around him in other stores, Hugo half whimsically admits a preference for Lamston's and Woolworth's: "They just place their merchandise very naturally in the window because they want to sell their three-dollar shirts. It's like the art of a child, very innocent. I would like to be able to do a window like that."

Other designers prefer to concentrate on the purely graphic presentation of fashion. To focus attention on clothes that convey a life of luxury and ease, Bonwit Teller's Cartledge used either strikingly realistic or anonymous mannequins without props or with very simple ones.

Candy Pratts, formerly of Bloomingdale's, is noted for a totally different approach. Playing out her fantasies in an entire block of windows, the twenty-seven-year-old Pratts created frozen moments for which the viewers provided imaginary actions for the inanimate participants. Her realistic and surrealistic tableaux, which incorporated strong emotions, violent dreams, and hints of masochism and sadism, gave Bloomingdale's a memorable cachet—and earned Pratts a reputation as the *enfant terrible* of the display world.

Candy Pratts is fashionable, original, attractive, self-confident, tough, and demanding. "I am what you see in my windows," she admits. "I am that experimental." Certain images—a still from an avant-garde film, a glass of wine spilling across a rug, the postures of an ecstatically dancing couple, the sudden turn of a jogger's head—appear and reappear in her work in one form or another. Her raw honesty combined with a desire to shock have resulted in memorable displays like the one hinting at suicide: A pair of legs, one of them encased in a high-heeled boot, hung suspended from the ceiling; the other boot lay forlornly on the floor, and a stark family portrait hung on the wall. Another notorious window depicted sexy female mannequins wearing Sonia Rykiel clothes sitting in a hotel lobby. Because the figures appeared to be enjoying one another's company and because no men were present, the scene caused a minor uproar among passersby who perceived strong homosexual implications in the situation. Pratts considered this reaction somewhat extreme. "At any given time," she explains, "there are only women sitting around at the nearby Barbizon Plaza Hotel, and no one thinks there's anything odd about that."

When Pratts designed Bloomingdale's Manhattan windows, the fourteen suburban branches duplicated her ideas in cookie-cutter fashion. Although the store's vice-president for fashion direction, Kal Ruttenstein, selected the clothes to be displayed, Pratts was under no obligation to clear her work with anyone except at Christmas, "because that's a big money venture." For Yuletide windows she presented a mock-up to Marvin Traub, Bloomingdale's trend-setting president. Acting on her belief that "clothes should speak for themselves," she never conferred with designers on the presentation of their creations.

"It's very easy to show beautiful clothes," Pratts acknowledged. "The greatest challenge is making a $19.95 suit look fabulous." Because strict union regulations prevented her from entering any of the forty windows in her domain, Pratts explained her concepts and exacting specifications to the staff of forty-five to fifty-five electricians, carpenters, painters, and window trimmers who construct rooms in Bloomingdale's own carpentry shop. When it was necessary she acted out her tableaux until the staff understood exactly what she wanted.

Considering the arresting, incomparable displays that Pratts designed for Charles Jourdan, and recalling her early work for Bloomingdale's, there is no disputing her statement, "I've toned down my windows." On the other hand, she added reflectively, "It's also possible that my audience caught up with me."

Another respected and widely imitated display designer is Bob Currie, a seminary-school dropout and former VISTA volunteer. As a free-lancer for Henri Bendel, he's obliged to please only Geraldine Stutz, the store's stylish president, and himself.

As a display director, Currie is in a position to create fashion. He remembers wrapping Indian silk turbans around the mannequins' heads before turbans were considered stylish and carefully burning the hems of a California designer's dresses to make them more exciting. "She used the same effect the following season," he adds. For another window he spontaneously linked raccoon-tail key rings with panty hose to create a stole; unaware of the ingenious way in which the accessory was put together, a fashion-conscious customer ordered one for herself. It was made up within the week by an obliging Bendel furrier.

Every Thursday evening (unless he's in Tokyo doing designer Hanae Mori's specialty shop windows), Currie creates flawlessly turned-out mannequins that are unquestionably the most dramatic in town. A workaholic, he makes the mannequins and clothes look as attractive as possible, then sets them in purposefully ambiguous situations. Although Currie dislikes offensive or violent images ("Why would you want to see more violence?"

he asks rhetorically.), he has occasionally produced windows that do reflect the dark side of life; one display featured a mannequin who looked clearly insane, while the other window showed a "dead" mannequin in equally beautiful attire clutching a bottle of pills.

Currie himself makes up the mannequins; several top models who have posed for him confide that he makes their doubles more beautiful than they are in reality. Meanwhile five assistants, including one woman, dress the figures. Working to disco music, the staff revs up on chocolates and coffee and, no matter how late, never loses its camaraderie.

Exacting in his demands on himself and others, Currie instructs assistants to "Put the sweater inside the skirt." "Add a wider bracelet." "Change the shade of the stockings." Then he'll dash across the main floor to the shoe department to choose styles more suitable than the ones already assembled. Upon his return he checks each assistant's work. Now, Currie brushes a mannequin's raven-black hair until it forms a rich halo, accents the collar of her jacket with a perfect poppy, fills in her mouth with amber lipstick. He may tell an assistant to put one mannequin's hands in her pockets or replace the limbs on another to achieve a more lifelike pose.

This week starkly dressed mannequins are posed among crates of oranges. Currie removes his shoes and steps onto the pristine white floor of the window. He rearranges the crates and the mannequins until they form a pleasing composition, cuts off a minuscule thread that no one else has noticed, adds another ebony bangle and sparkling jet-black comb, and orders one of the free-lance lighting experts to soften one mannequin's face.

Currie often adds an element of humor to his windows "to make it easier for customers to spend a serious amount of money and to take the edge off for those who can't afford to." He once placed menacing-looking, fur-coated mannequins with hatchets stuck in their belts among stacks of wood "as relief from Fendi's pricey coats." Even though props are chosen in advance, he may not decide how to use them to best advantage until he is standing in the window. Last Halloween, pumpkins spray-painted gold were set on the floor. At the last minute Currie realized that it would be far more amusing to place them over the mannequins' heads.

Currie's admirers make it a point to walk on Bendel's side of Fifty-seventh Street to be entertained and delighted by his creations. One week several superthin mannequins languidly rested on a voluptuous chaise longue; another time ravishing creatures with spaghetti-encrusted hair posed next to champagne-filled refrigerators. These windows were entitled "Home on the Range."

Display designers, like fashion designers, employ creativity in the interests of moving merchandise. As an ideal stage for freezing fantasies and projecting illusions, store windows of the 1970s have glamorized the need to buy in the service of fashion's need to sell.

INDEX

ROSE HARTMAN is a free-lance journalist and photographer based in New York City. She was born in Manhattan, attended Hunter College High School, and studied English at City College of New York. In addition, she has studied painting, photography, dance, and art history. For twelve years Ms. Hartman taught English on the high school level in the New York City public schools. She has worked and traveled extensively in Europe and South America. Her fascination with the fashion world was sparked at an early age when she read *Vogue* and *Bazaar* at the library and strolled by the windows on Fifth Avenue. She has photographed and reported on all aspects of the fashion scene—from the shows and parties to the personalities and styles. "For me, fashion's luster has never faded."